TWENTY FIRST CENTURY
science

GCSE
Additional
Science

Philippa Gardom Hulme

OXFORD
UNIVERSITY PRESS

OXFORD
UNIVERSITY PRESS

Great Clarendon Street, Oxford OX2 6DP

Oxford University Press is a department of the University of Oxford.
It furthers the University's objective of excellence in research, scholarship,
and education by publishing worldwide in

Oxford   New York

Auckland   Cape Town   Dar es Salaam   Hong Kong   Karachi
Kuala Lumpur   Madrid   Melbourne   Mexico City   Nairobi
New Delhi   Shanghai   Taipei   Toronto

With offices in

Argentina   Austria   Brazil   Chile   Czech Republic   France   Greece
Guatemala   Hungary   Italy   Japan   Poland   Portugal   Singapore
South Korea   Switzerland   Thailand   Turkey   Ukraine   Vietnam

British Library Cataloguing in Publication Data

Data available

ISBN-13: 9780199152346

10 9 8 7 6 5 4

Printed in Great Britain Bell and Bain Ltd Glasgow

Author Acknowledgements
Thanks to Barney for all the ideas and constructive criticism. Thanks to Mum for some of the puzzles, and Mum and
Dad for help with checking. Thanks to Catherine and Sarah for keeping out of the study – and to Barney, Mum, Dad
and Helen for keeping them happy!

Acknowledgements
These resources have been developed to support teachers and students undertaking a new OCR suite of GCSE
Science specifications, Twenty First Century Science.

Many people from schools, colleges, universities, industry, and the professions have contributed to the
production of these resources. The feedback from over 75 Pilot Centres was invaluable. It led to significant
changes to the course specifications, and to the supporting resources for teaching and learning.

The University of York Science Education Group (UYSEG) and Nuffield Curriculum Centre worked in partnership
with an OCR team led by Mary Whitehouse, Elizabeth Herbert and Emily Clare to create the specifications,
which have their origins in the Beyond 2000 report (Millar & Osborne, 1998) and subsequent Key Stage 4
development work undertaken by UYSEG and the Nuffield Curriculum Centre for QCA. Bryan Milner and Michael
Reiss also contributed to this work, which is reported in: 21st Century Science GCSE Pilot Development: Final
Report (UYSEG, March 2002).

Sponsors
The development of Twenty First Century Science was made possible by generous support from:
• The Nuffield Foundation
• The Salter's Institute
• The Wellcome Trust

THE SALTERS' INSTITUTE

Contents

About this book

To parents and carers

This book is designed to help students achieve their best in OCR's Twenty First Century Additional Science GCSE examination. It includes sections on each of the areas of biology, chemistry, and physics explored by Twenty First Century Science.

This book is designed to be used! Students will get the most from it if they do as many of the Workout and GCSE-style questions as possible. Many students will also find it helpful to highlight, colour, and scribble extra notes in the Fact banks.

To students

This book is in nine sections. There is one section for each of the biology, chemistry, and physics modules B4 to P6.

Each section includes:

Workout

Go through these on your own or with a friend. Write your answers in the book. If you get stuck, look in the Fact bank. The index will help you to find what you need. Check your answers at the back of the book.

Fact bank

Each fact bank summarizes information from the module in just six pages. Don't just read the Fact banks – highlight key points, scribble extra details in the margin or on sticky notes, and make up ways to help you remember things. The messier this book is by the time you take your exams, the better!

You could try getting a friend – or someone at home – to test you on the Fact banks. Or make cards to test yourself. These could have

- a question on one side and an answer on the other or
- a word on one side and its definition on the other

GCSE-style questions

These are very like the module test questions. There are also two questions (question 3 in module B4 and question 3 in P6) that are similar to questions on the Ideas in Context paper. All the answers are at the back of the book.

In every section, content required for Higher level only is shown like this: **H**

Chemical data such as proton numbers and relative atomic masses can be found in the **periodic table** on page 31.

Skills assessment: investigation

Turn to pages 166–167 for a summary of essential advice on maximizing your marks in the investigation assessment task.

Workout   B4 Homeostasis

1 Next to each activity, write down one or more things affected by the activity.

Choose words and phrases from the box.

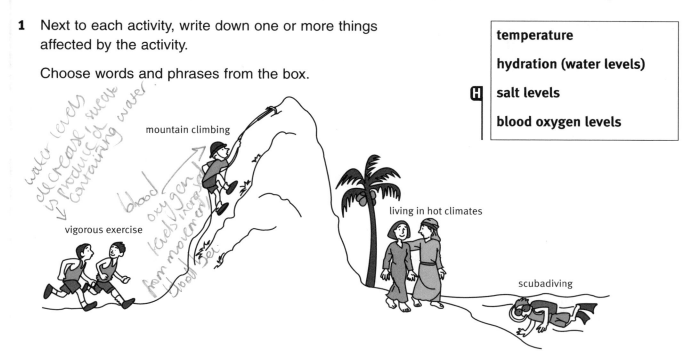

water levels decrease & sweat is produced of containing water

mountain climbing

blood oxygen levels increase from movement blood flex

vigorous exercise

living in hot climates

scubadiving

| temperature |
| hydration (water levels) |
| salt levels |
| blood oxygen levels |

2 Draw lines to match
 ▸ each part of a control system in the body to its purpose **and**
 ▸ each purpose to a part of a premature baby's incubator

Part of an automatic control system in the body	Purpose	Part of artificial temperature control system in an incubator
receptor	to produce the response	thermostat with a switch
processing centre	to detect stimuli	heater
effector	to receive information and coordinate responses	temperature sensor

3 Fill in the gaps to show what enzymes do and how they work.

Enzymes are ___protein___ molecules that ___speed___ ___up___ chemical reactions in cells.
Enzymes work best at ___37___ °C in humans.

 ▸ At lower temperatures, the reaction is too ___slow___ because
 ___there are less collisions between enzymes + molecules___

 ▸ At higher temperatures, enzymes stop working.
 They are ___denatured___.
 This happens because ___the shape of the active site in___
 ___the lock + key has changed.___

Every type of enzyme has a particular shape and speeds up a particular reaction. The molecules that take part in the reaction must be shaped to fit the enzyme's shape. The molecules bind to the enzyme at the ___active site___. This is the ___lock___ ___+___ ___key___ model.

4 Look at captions **A** to **G**. Write one letter in each box to show what happens in each part of the body's temperature control system. Use each letter once or twice.

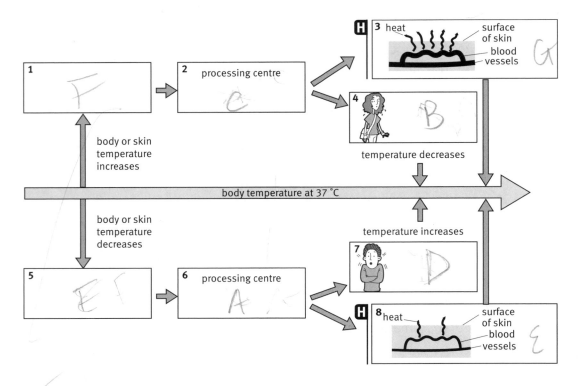

6 A The brain (hypothalamus)

▶ sends nerve impulses that cause muscle cells to contract quickly
▶ sends impulses to muscles in blood vessel walls

B Sweat glands make more sweat. Sweat evaporates, taking heat from the body.

2 C The brain (hypothalamus)

▶ sends more nerve impulses to sweat glands
▶ stops sending impulses to muscles in blood vessel walls

D Muscles in cells contract quickly. Cells respire faster and more heat is released.

E Muscles in blood vessel walls contract. Blood vessels get narrower. Less energy transferred as heat from body surface.

F Temperature receptors in the skin or brain detect this change.

G Muscles in blood vessel walls relax. Blood vessels get wider. More energy transferred as heat from body surface.

5 Finish the doctor's speech bubbles.

6 Finish the rescuer's speech bubbles.

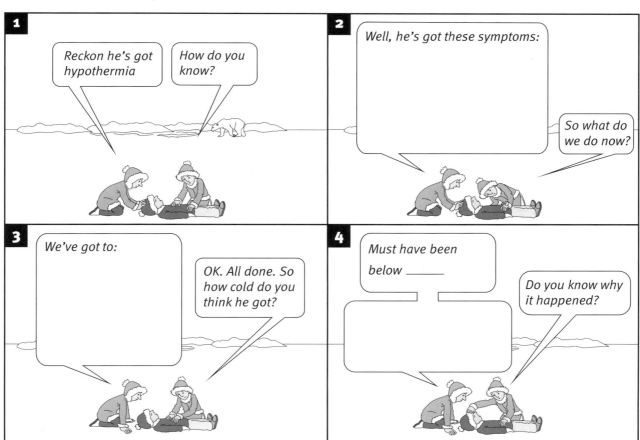

7 Write **O** next to the sentences that apply to osmosis.
Write **D** next to the sentences that apply to diffusion.

Ⓗ Write **A** next to the sentences that apply to active transport.

You may write more than one letter next to a sentence.

a This process does not need energy. _____

b In this process, liquid or gas molecules move
from an area of high concentration (where there
are many of them) to an area of low
concentration (where there are fewer of them). _____

c In this process, molecules enter and/or leave a cell
through the cell's partially permeable membrane. _____

d Carbon dioxide leaves cells by this process. _____

e This is a passive process. _____

f Oxygen enters cells by this process. _____

g In this process, water molecules go through a
partially permeable membrane from a dilute
solution to a concentrated solution. _____

Ⓗ **h** In this process, molecules move from a region
where they are at low concentration to a region
where they are at high concentration. _____

i This process uses energy from respiration to
get molecules across the cell membrane. _____

8 a Annotate the picture to show

▸ three ways that water enters the body
▸ fours ways that water leaves the body

Ⓗ **b** Complete the sentences.

▸ If too much water gets into an animal cell,

_____

_____

▸ If too much water leaves an animal cell,

_____

_____

9 The stages below describe how urine is made and removed from the body. They are in the wrong order.

A The remaining liquid is sent to the bladder. This urine contains urea, water and salt.

B The urine is excreted from the body.

C The kidneys filter out small molecules (urea, water, glucose, and salt) from the blood.

D The urine is stored in the bladder.

E Molecules the body needs are reabsorbed.

Fill in the boxes to show the correct order.

☐ ☐ ☐ ☐ ☐

10 Write **T** next to the sentences that are true.
Write **F** next to the sentences that are false.

a The kidneys filter small molecules out of the blood. ☐

b After exercise your kidneys make less urine than if you had not exercised. ☐

c The kidneys reabsorb all the glucose back into the blood. ☐

d Drinking alcohol makes a person's urine more dilute than normal. ☐

e The kidneys reabsorb all the salt back into the blood. ☐

f Drinking alcohol makes a person excrete a smaller volume of urine than normal. ☐

g On hot days, your kidneys make more urine than on cold days. ☐

h Taking Ecstasy leads to concentrated urine. ☐

i After taking Ecstasy, a smaller volume of urine is made. ☐

j Taking Ecstasy stops the pituitary gland releasing ADH. ☐

k Alcohol makes the pituitary gland release more ADH. ☐

H **11** Look at captions **A** to **L** below. Write one letter in each box to show how water balance is controlled in the body.

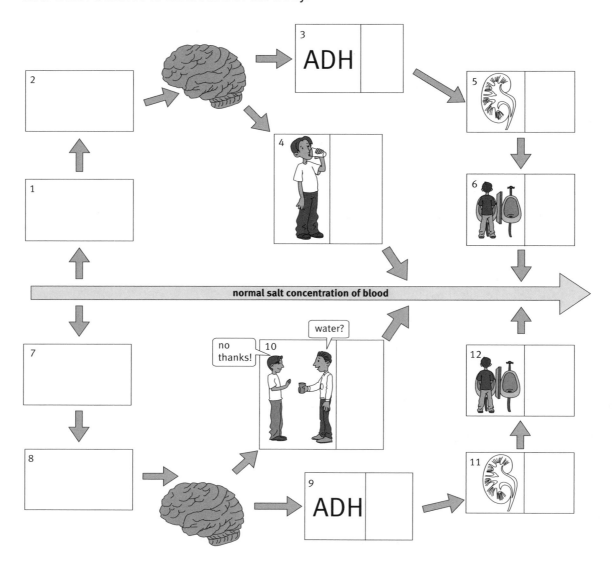

A The concentration of salt in the blood increases.

B The concentration of salt in the blood decreases.

C Receptors in the brain's hypothalamus detect that salt concentrations are too high.

D The hypothalamus causes the pituitary gland to release the hormone ADH into the blood stream.

E The ADH travels in the blood to the kidneys. More water is reabsorbed.

F Less urine is made. It is more concentrated.

G Receptors in the brain's hypothalamus detect that salt concentrations are too low.

H The hypothalamus causes the pituitary gland to release less ADH into the blood stream.

I The ADH travels to tubules in the kidneys. Less water is reabsorbed.

J More urine is made. It is more dilute.

K The person feels thirsty and drinks water.

L The person does not feel thirsty and drinks less water.

What is homeostasis?

Cells work properly only if conditions are correct, like temperature and water level. Automatic control systems keep body conditions constant. Keeping a constant internal environment is called **homeostasis**.

Body control systems are similar to artificial control systems. They have

▶ **receptors** to detect stimuli
▶ **processing centres** to receive information and coordinate responses
▶ **effectors** to produce responses

A baby incubator is an artificial control system. It has a temperature sensor, a thermostat with a switch, and a heater.

▶ The sensor detects the temperature. If it is cooler than 32 °C, the thermostat switches on the heater.

▶ The thermostat switches off the heater when the temperature rises back to 32 °C.

[H] In a control system, any change leads to an action that reverses the change. **Negative feedback** between the effector and the receptor makes this happen.

[H] Some effectors have opposite effects to each other. They work **antagonistically**. This makes the response very sensitive.

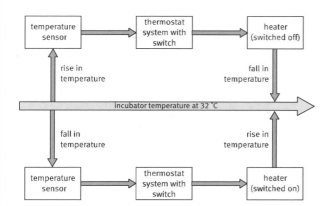

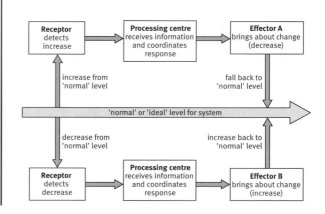

The table shows how activities affect homeostasis.

Activity	What it affects
strenuous exercise	temperature, hydration (water levels), [H] salt levels, [H] blood oxygen levels
surviving in hot or cold climates	temperature, hydration, [H] salt levels
[H] scuba diving	blood oxygen levels
mountain climbing	blood oxygen levels

Enzymes

Enzymes speed up chemical reactions in cells. Enzymes work best in certain conditions. This is an important reason for keeping cell conditions constant.

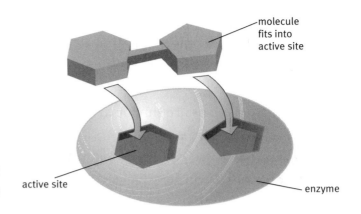

molecule fits into active site

active site

enzyme

Enzymes are protein molecules. Every type of enzyme has a different shape and speeds up a particular reaction. The molecules that take part in the reaction must fit exactly into the enzyme's **active site**. This is the **lock and key model**.

Enzymes in humans work best at 37 °C.

▶ Below 37 °C there are few collisions between enzyme molecules and reacting molecules. Reactions are too slow.

▶ At 37 °C collisions happen more often. Collisions also have more energy. So the reaction is faster.

▶ Above 37 °C, enzymes don't work. They **denature**.

H When an enzyme denatures the shape of the active site changes. Molecules no longer fit into the active site, so the reaction cannot happen. Changes in pH cause the same problem.

Keeping body temperature constant

Your body temperature must stay at 37 °C. **Respiration** releases energy from your food for your body to use. You may also gain energy from your environment, if it is hotter than you. Your body must balance energy gain and energy loss to keep a constant temperature.

The body's **core** is warmer than its **extremities** (for example hands and feet). At the core, energy is transferred to the blood. At the extremities, blood transfers energy to tissues.

The body's temperature control system includes

▶ temperature receptors in the skin to detect the temperature outside the body

▶ temperature receptors in the brain to detect the blood's temperature (**H** in the hypothalamus)

▶ a processing centre in the brain (**H** in the hypothalamus) which receives information from receptors and triggers responses in effectors

▶ effectors, for example sweat glands and muscles

At high body temperatures, the body cools down by

▶ making **sweat**. When sweat evaporates, energy is transferred from skin to sweat.

H ▶ **vasodilation**. Blood vessels that supply the skin's capillaries get wider. So more blood flows through the capillaries and the body loses more energy.

At low body temperatures, the body warms up by

▶ **shivering**, which happens when muscles contract fast. Respiration in the muscle cells increases. Respiration releases some energy as heat to nearby tissues.

▶ **vasoconstriction**. Blood vessels that supply the skin's capillaries get narrower. So less blood flows through the capillaries and the body loses less energy.

Vasodilation and vasoconstriction are examples of effectors that work **antagonistically** (they are opposites). Their response is very sensitive.

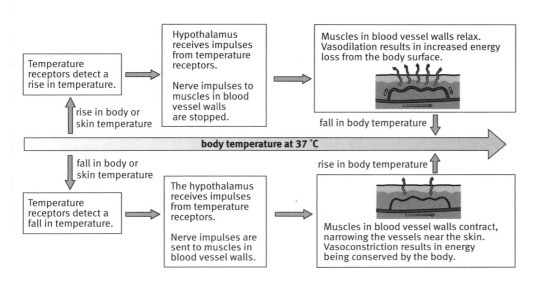

Heat stroke and hypothermia

	Heat stroke	Hypothermia
What is it?	when core body temperature rises above 42 °C	when core body temperature falls below 35 °C
Symptoms and causes	▶ hot, dry skin because sweating stops ▶ fast pulse rate because of dehydration and stress ▶ dizziness and confusion because nerve cells in the brain are damaged	▶ shivering, confusion, slurred speech, loss of co-ordination ▶ coma below 30 °C ▶ death below 28 °C
Treatment	▶ sponge with water ▶ put near a fan ▶ put ice under arms and in groin	▶ insulate the patient ▶ warm gently with warm towels ▶ give warm drinks
Other points	When it is very hot, you sweat more. This may cause dehydration. When you're dehydrated you sweat less, so your body temperature rises out of control. The body's normal methods of temperature control no longer work	body loses energy faster than it gains energy

Getting substances into and out of cells

Liquid and gas molecules move randomly all the time. Overall, they move from an area of high concentration (where there are many of them) to an area of low concentration (where there are fewer of them). This is **diffusion**. It is a **passive** process – it does not need energy.

Cell membranes are **partially permeable**. Water molecules can get through their small holes. Overall, more water molecules diffuse through partially permeable membranes from a dilute solution (with many water molecules) to a more concentrated solution (with fewer water molecules). This is **osmosis**.

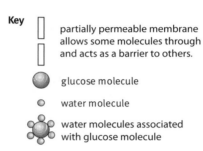

Key

⬜ partially permeable membrane allows some molecules through and acts as a barrier to others.

⬤ glucose molecule

○ water molecule

⬤ water molecules associated with glucose molecule

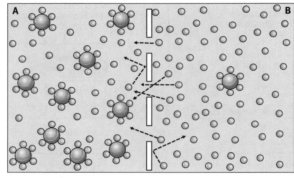

Overall, water molecules move from right (B) to left (A). This is osmosis.

Other chemicals (such as carbon dioxide, oxygen, and dissolved food molecules) also diffuse through partially permeable cell membranes.

H Sometimes a cell needs to take in molecules (such as glucose) that have a higher concentration inside the cell than outside it. The cell uses **active transport** to do this. Respiration provides energy for active transport.

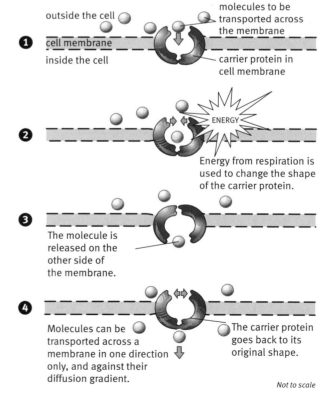

How molecules are moved across a cell membrane by active transport.

Controlling water levels

Cells only work properly if the concentrations of their contents are correct.

H If too much water moves into an animal cell, the cell membrane may rupture (break).

If too much water moves out of an animal cell, the solutions in the cell become too concentrated. The cell cannot work properly.

Your body loses and gains water to keep water levels balanced.

Your kidneys control water levels. They also get rid of waste products by **excretion**.

Kidneys work like this:

▶ They filter out small molecules from the blood (urea, water, glucose, and salt). Blood cells and protein molecules stay in the blood.

▶ They send all the urea, and some water and salt, to the bladder. This is **urine**. It is stored in the bladder and later excreted.

▶ They **reabsorb** molecules that the body needs – including all the glucose and some water and salt – back into the blood.

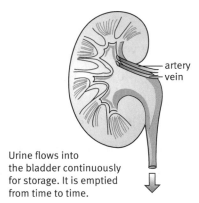

Urine flows into the bladder continuously for storage. It is emptied from time to time.

Cross-section through a kidney

Kidneys control water levels by making different amounts of urine. On hot days you sweat more. So your kidneys make less urine. You also make less urine after exercise, if you've not drunk much water, or if you've eaten salty food.

H Kidneys are part of a **negative feedback system**.

▶ **Receptors** in the hypothalamus detect changes in salt concentration in blood plasma.

▶ If salt concentrations are too high, the **processing centre** (hypothalamus) makes the **pituitary gland** release **ADH** (a hormone) into the bloodstream.

▶ The ADH travels to the kidneys (**effectors**). The more ADH that arrives, the more water the kidneys reabsorb. So the more concentrated the urine.

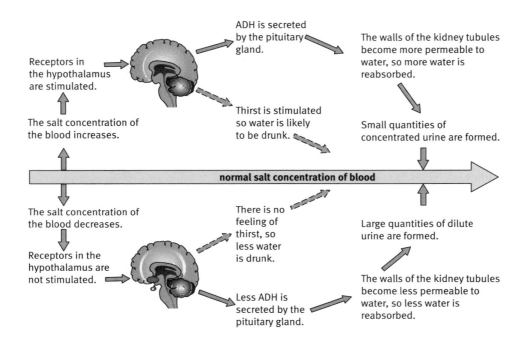

ADH is secreted by the pituitary gland.

The walls of the kidney tubules become more permeable to water, so more water is reabsorbed.

Receptors in the hypothalamus are stimulated.

Thirst is stimulated so water is likely to be drunk.

The salt concentration of the blood increases.

Small quantities of concentrated urine are formed.

normal salt concentration of blood

The salt concentration of the blood decreases.

There is no feeling of thirst, so less water is drunk.

Large quantities of dilute urine are formed.

Receptors in the hypothalamus are not stimulated.

Less ADH is secreted by the pituitary gland.

The walls of the kidney tubules become less permeable to water, so less water is reabsorbed.

Drugs affect the amount of urine you make:

▶ Drinking alcohol leads to big volumes of dilute urine, so you may get dehydrated.

H This is because alcohol stops the pituitary gland releasing ADH.

▶ Taking Ecstasy leads to small volumes of concentrated urine.

H This is because Ecstasy makes the pituitary gland release more ADH.

1 Premature babies are put in incubators.
An incubator is an artificial temperature control system.

a Draw a line to match each part of the incubator to the part of the human body that does a similar job.

Part of incubator	Part of human body that does a similar job
temperature sensor	sweat glands
heater (switched on)	skin
thermostat with a switch	muscle cells (contracting quickly to cause shivering)
heater (switched off)	brain

[3]

b **i** A **negative feedback system** controls the temperature of an incubator.

Which statement below **best** describes a negative feedback system?
Put a tick in the **one** correct box.

If there is a change in the system, the system responds immediately. ☐

If there is a change in the system, the system measures the effect of the change. ☐

If there is a change in the system, there is an action that increases the change. ☑

If there is a change in the system, there is an action that reverses the change. ☐

[1]

ii **Antagonistic effectors** control the temperature of a human body.

Give **one advantage** of a control system having two antagonistic effectors.

They are prepared for more then one circumstance.

[1]

Total [5]

2 Catalase is an enzyme. It speeds up the breakdown of poisonous hydrogen peroxide molecules. The reaction happens in liver cells.

a What type of chemical is catalase?

Draw a (ring) around the correct answer.

fat   **carbohydrate**   **vitamin**   (**protein**)   [1]

b Hydrogen peroxide molecules break down to make water and oxygen. The word equation for the reaction is below.

hydrogen peroxide → water + oxygen

Daniel does an experiment. He wants to find out how temperature affects the rate of this reaction.

He sets up the apparatus shown.

He drops a small piece of chicken liver into each test tube. Chicken liver contains catalase.

Frothy bubbles form above the liquid. The froth contains oxygen gas.

Daniel measures the highest point that the froth gets to after 30 seconds.

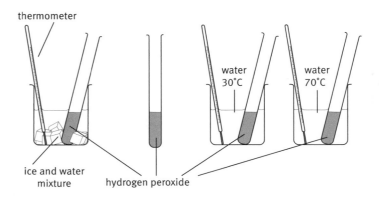

His results are below.

Temperature (°C)	0	20	30	70
Height of froth (cm)	0.5	2	2.5	0

i Which of the following statements **best** explains why the reaction was faster at 30 °C than at 20 °C? Tick one box.

At 30 °C collisions between catalase and hydrogen peroxide are less frequent. ☐

At 30 °C collisions between catalase and hydrogen peroxide have more energy. ☐

At 30 °C collisions between catalase and hydrogen peroxide are more frequent and have more energy. ☑

At 30 °C collisions between catalase and hydrogen peroxide have more energy and are less frequent. ☐   [1]

ii Daniel saw no bubbles at 70 °C.

What has happened to the enzyme?

_____   [1]

c Below is a schematic diagram of a hydrogen peroxide molecule.

Which drawing represents the enzyme catalase?

Put a (ring) around the correct answer.

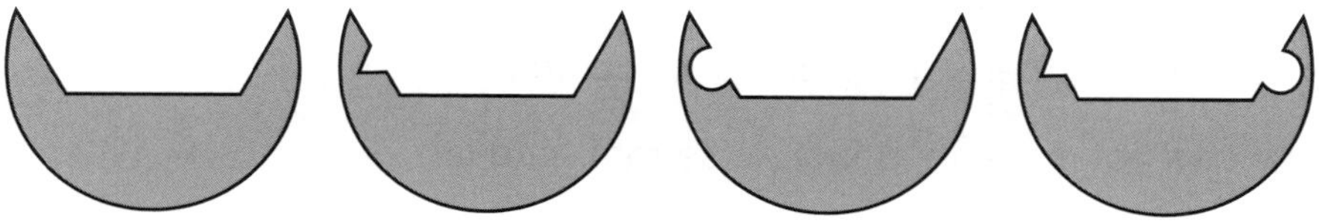

A   B   C   D   [1]

H d i Give the name of the part of an enzyme where reactions occur.

_____ [1]

ii If the pH is too high or too low, catalase does not speed up the breakdown of hydrogen peroxide molecules.

Explain why.

_____

_____

_____

_____ [2]

Total [7]

3

In 2003, a heat wave killed 30 000 people in Europe.

Many of the people who died were elderly. Scientists say that this is partly because elderly people are slower to detect high temperatures. So they are slower to do things that will help them cool down.

A person suffers heatstroke when the brain reaches 38.5 °C. The hypothalamus is damaged and their temperature control system fails. They no longer sweat and their temperature rises out of control.

A person with heatstroke has hot dry skin, a fast pulse rate, and is dizzy and confused.

Scientists advise preventing heatstroke by

▶ drinking lots of water
▶ staying inside at the hottest time of day
▶ getting cool at night
▶ avoiding alcohol

In another heat wave, in 2006, Italian emergency workers tried to prevent heatstroke by handing out water to people waiting in the sun for buses.

Doctors advise treating someone with heatstroke by

▶ sponging with cool water
▶ putting cool flannels on the face and neck

It is dangerous to throw lots of cold water over a person with heatstroke. This makes the body think it is losing too much heat, so it shuts down the circulation to the skin. That means that all the hot blood in the body is diverted towards the brain.

a Give **two** symptoms of heatstroke.

_____

_____ [2]

b Which part of the body's temperature control system works less well in old people than in young people, according to the article?

Draw a (ring) around the correct answer.

sensors   **processing centre**   **effectors** [1]

c Explain why drinking plenty of water helps to prevent heatstroke.

_____

_____

_____ [2]

d Suggest why cooling down properly at night helps to prevent heatstroke.

_____

_____

_____ [2]

e A person who has heatstroke stops sweating.

Explain why this is a problem.

One mark is for writing in sentences with correct spelling, punctuation, and grammar.

_____

_____

_____

_____ [2+1]

f **i** Which part of the temperature control system does alcohol interfere with?

Draw a (ring) around the correct answer.

sensors   **processing centre**   **effectors** [1]

ii Suggest another reason why doctors advise avoiding alcohol to prevent heatstroke.

_____

_____

_____ [1]

H

g Explain why it is dangerous to throw cold water over a heatstroke victim.

_____

_____

_____ [2]

Total [14]

4 This question is about how chemicals move into and out of animal cells.

a Name two chemicals that move into or out of animal cells by diffusion.

_____   _____

[2]

b **i** Which of the following statements **best** describes osmosis?

Tick one box.

Molecules move from a region of their high concentration
to a region of their low concentration through a partially
permeable membrane.   ☐

Molecules move from a region of their low concentration
to a region of their high concentration through a partially
permeable membrane.   ☐

Water molecules move from a dilute solution to a
concentrated solution through a partially permeable
membrane.   ☐

Water molecules move from a concentrated solution to a
dilute solution through a partially permeable membrane.   ☐   [1]

ii What can happen if too much water moves into an animal cell?

_____

[1]

c The table shows the concentration of ions of two chemicals inside
and outside a cell.

Ion	Relative concentration inside cell	Relative concentration outside cell
Na^+	10	143
K^+	140	5

Draw a line to match each substance to how it gets into the cell.

Substance
Na^+ ion
K^+ ion
water molecule

How it gets into the cell
osmosis
active transport
diffusion

[2]

Total [6]

This page is blank.

This page is blank.

1 a Fill in column B of the table below. Choose words from the box.

| harmful | toxic | irritant | corrosive | oxidizing | highly flammable |

b In column C, write down one safety precaution you must take when using a chemical that displays the hazard symbol. (Assume you are already wearing eye protection.)

A Hazard symbol	B Meaning of symbol	C Safety precaution
✖		
☠		
🔥		

2 Write the symbol of each element in the box below its proton number. You can find these in the periodic table on page 31.

Proton number	3	56	53	16	9	92	7	16	8	53	16	75	23	53	14	8	7
Symbol	Li					U											

Now crack the code. What does the sentence say?

_____

3 Join the dots to make a picture.

Start at the element with the lowest relative atomic mass. Join this to the element with the next lowest relative atomic mass, and so on.

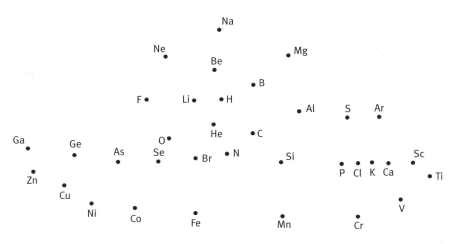

4 Write the symbol of each element in the box below its relative atomic mass. You can find this information in the periodic table on page 31.

Relative atomic mass	32	4	127	32	9	197	48	19	238	7	232	127	14	39
Symbol									U		Th			

Now crack the code. What does the sentence say?

_____

5 On the periodic table:

▶ colour in red the group that includes the element calcium
▶ colour in blue the period that includes the element phosphorus
▶ colour in pencil all the non-metals
▶ circle in red **three** elements that form ions with a charge of +1
▶ circle in blue **three** elements that form ions with a charge of −2

period number	1	2											3	4	5	6	7	8
1	H																	He
2	Li	Be											B	C	N	O	F	Ne
3	Na	Mg											Al	Si	P	S	Cl	Ar
4	K	Ca	Sc	Ti	V	Cr	Mn	Fe	Co	Ni	Cu	Zn	Ga	Ge	As	Se	Br	Kr
5	Rb	Sr	Y	Zr	Nb	Mo	Tc	Ru	Rh	Pd	Ag	Cd	In	Sn	Sb	Te	I	Xe
6	Cs	Ba	La	Hf	Ta	W	Re	Os	Ir	Pt	Au	Hg	Tl	Pb	Bi	Po	At	Rn
7	Fr	Ra	Ac															

group number

6 Write the missing **number** or **symbol** of an element in each sentence below. (Use the periodic table on page 31 to help you.)

a The mass of a carbon atom is _____ times the mass of a helium atom.

b The mass of a silicon atom is twice the mass of a _____ atom.

c The mass of a bromine atom is _____ times the mass of a neon atom.

d The mass of an atom of _____ is twice the mass of a silicon atom.

e The mass of a gallium atom is five times the mass of a _____ atom.

7 For the sentences below

▶ write **1** next to each sentence that is true for **group 1**
▶ write **7** next to each sentence that is true for **group 7**
▶ write **B** next to each sentence that is true for both **group 7 and group 8**

You will need the data in the table to help you answer some of the questions.

Element	Boiling point (°C)	Density (g/cm³)
lithium	1347	0.53
sodium	883	0.97
potassium	774	0.86
chlorine	−34	1.56
bromine	59	3.1
iodine	184	4.9

a Going down this group, boiling point increases. ☐

b Going up this group, the elements get more reactive. ☐

c The elements in this group are bleaches. ☐

d Going up this group, proton number decreases. ☐

e The elements in this group react with water to make hydrogen gas. ☐

f Atoms of the elements in this group form diatomic molecules. ☐

g The elements in this group tarnish quickly in damp air. ☐

h Going down this group, density increases. ☐

i Going down this group, boiling point decreases. ☐

j All the atoms of the elements in this group have the same number of electrons in the outermost shell. ☐

k The elements at the top of this group are gases. ☐

l Going down the group, the colours of the elements get darker. ☐

8 Complete the word equations.

a sodium + water → sodium hydroxide + _____

b potassium + chlorine → _____ _____

c hydrogen + _____ → hydrogen iodide

d lithium + _____ → lithium hydroxide + _____

e sodium + _____ → _____ chloride

f lithium + _____ → lithium bromide

9 Fill in the empty boxes.

Name	Formula
water	
hydrogen gas	
	KBr
sodium hydroxide	
	LiI
chlorine gas	

H 10 Balance the equations. Then add state symbols to show the states of the reactants at room temperature and pressure.

a K + H_2O → KOH + H_2

b Na + Cl_2 → $NaCl$

c Li + H_2O → $LiOH$ + H_2

d Cl_2 + K → KCl

e Fe + Cl_2 → $FeCl_3$

11 Write **Q** next to the pair of elements which react most vigorously at room temperature.

Write **S** next to the pair of elements which react most slowly. (Leave the other boxes blank.)

sodium and bromine ☐

lithium and chlorine ☐

sodium and iodine ☐

potassium and chlorine ☐

lithium and iodine ☐

12 Draw crosses on the circles to show how the electrons are arranged in atoms of these elements. (Hint: not all of the shells will contain electrons.)

lithium

beryllium

carbon

fluorine

sodium

phosphorus

chlorine

argon

13 Use words from the box to fill in the gaps.
Use each word once, more than once, or not at all.

Atoms have a small central _____. This is made of

protons and _____. Electrons are arranged in _____ round

the nucleus. In a neutral atom, the number of _____ is equal to the

number of protons. The way an element reacts depends on how its

_____ are arranged.

The halogens have similar reactions to each other because they all have

_____ electrons in the outermost shell.

shells
electrons
nucleus
neutrons
7
protons
2

14 Draw lines to match each statement with the best reason.

Statement	Reason
Solid ionic compounds form crystals	because it forms when an atom loses an electron
The charge on a sodium ion is +1	because it forms when an atom gains an electron
The charge on a bromide ion is −1	because their ions are arranged in a regular lattice
Liquid ionic compounds conduct electricity	because their ions are free to move
Ionic compounds conduct electricity when they are dissolved in water	because their ions are not free to move
Solid ionic compounds do not conduct electricity	because their ions are free to move

29

15 Fill in the empty boxes below. (Use the periodic table on page 31 to help you.)

	Chlorine atom	Iodide ion	Potassium ion	Lithium atom	Bromide ion	Lithium ion	Sodium atom
Symbol of atom or ion		I⁻		Li			
Number of protons	17		19		35		11
Number of electrons		54		3		2	

⒣ 16 Use the information in the table to work out the formulae of the compounds below.

Positive ions	Negative ions
Na⁺	Cl⁻
K⁺	Br⁻
Mg²⁺	O²⁻
Ca²⁺	S²⁻

a Sodium bromide   _____

b Potassium chloride   _____

c Magnesium sulfide   _____

d Potassium oxide   _____

e Calcium oxide   _____

f Calcium bromide   _____

17 Use the information in the table from question 16 to help you answer the questions below.

a The formula of strontium oxide is SrO.
What is the charge on the strontium ion?   _____

b The formula of beryllium chloride is $BeCl_2$.
What is the charge on the beryllium ion?   _____

c The formula of rubidium chloride is RbCl.
What is the charge on the rubidium ion?   _____

d The formula of strontium oxide is Cs_2O.
What is the charge on the caesium ion?   _____

The periodic table

period number	1	2											3	4	5	6	7	8
1	1 H hydrogen 1						group number											4 He helium 2
2	7 Li lithium 3	9 Be beryllium 4											11 B boron 5	12 C carbon 6	14 N nitrogen 7	16 O oxygen 8	19 F fluorine 9	20 Ne neon 10
3	23 Na sodium 11	24 Mg magnesium 12											27 Al aluminium 13	28 Si silicon 14	31 P phosphorus 15	32 S sulfur 16	35.5 Cl chlorine 17	40 Ar argon 18
4	39 K potassium 19	40 Ca calcium 20	45 Sc scandium 21	48 Ti titanium 22	51 V vanadium 23	52 Cr chromium 24	55 Mn manganese 25	56 Fe iron 26	59 Co cobalt 27	59 Ni nickel 28	63.5 Cu copper 29	65 Zn zinc 30	70 Ga gallium 31	73 Ge germanium 32	75 As arsenic 33	79 Se selenium 34	80 Br bromine 35	84 Kr krypton 36
5	86 Rb rubidium 37	88 Sr strontium 38	89 Y yttrium 39	91 Zr zirconium 40	93 Nb niobium 41	96 Mo molybdenum 42	97 Tc technetium 43	101 Ru ruthenium 44	103 Rh rhodium 45	106 Pd palladium 46	108 Ag silver 47	112 Cd cadmium 48	115 In indium 49	119 Sn tin 50	122 Sb antimony 51	128 Te tellurium 52	127 I iodine 53	131 Xe xenon 54
6	133 Cs caesium 55	137 Ba barium 56	139 La lanthanum 57	179 Hf hafnium 72	181 Ta tantalum 73	184 W tungsten 74	186 Re rhenium 75	190 Os osmium 76	192 Ir iridium 77	195 Pt platinum 78	197 Au gold 79	201 Hg mercury 80	204 Tl thallium 81	207 Pb lead 82	209 Bi bismuth 83	210 Po polonium 84	210 At astatine 85	222 Rn radon 86
7	223 Fr francium 87	226 Ra radium 88	227 Ac actinium 89	104	105	106	107	108	109	110	111	112						

The elements are arranged in order of **proton number**. There are repeating patterns in the elements' properties.

The vertical columns are **groups**. The elements of a group have similar properties.

The horizontal rows are **periods**.

Key

210 — relative atomic mass
Po — symbol
Polonium — name
84 — proton number

□ metals
▨ non-metals

Chemical safety

Symbol	Meaning	Safety precautions Wear eye protection and . . .
☠	**Toxic** – can cause death if absorbed by skin, swallowed or breathed in	▸ wear gloves ▸ work in fume cupboard or wear mask over mouth and nose
✖	**Harmful** – like toxic substances, but less dangerous	▸ wash off spills quickly ▸ use in a well-ventilated room
🧪	**Corrosive** – attacks living tissue, like eyes or skin	▸ wear gloves
✖	**Irritant** – makes skin red or blistered	▸ wash off spills quickly
🔥	**Highly flammable** – catches fire easily	▸ keep away from flames, sparks and oxidizing chemicals
🔥	**Oxidizing** – provides oxygen so other chemicals burn more fiercely	▸ keep away from flammable chemicals

Patterns in the properties of elements

Group 1: the alkali metals

Lithium   Li

Sodium   Na   and

Potassium   K   and

Alkali metals

▸ float on water – they have **low densities**
▸ have **low melting** and **boiling points**
▸ are **shiny** when freshly cut
▸ quickly **tarnish** in damp air

Alkali metals react with water to make **hydrogen** and an **alkaline solution**.

For example:

sodium + water → hydrogen + sodium hydroxide

$2Na(s) + 2H_2O(l) \rightarrow H_2(g) + 2NaOH(aq)$

Reacting sodium with water. Universal indicator solution in the trough changes from green to purple.

Going down the group, the reactions get **more vigorous.**

Metal	Observation
lithium	▸ lithium floats and fizzes gently
sodium	▸ sodium melts and whizzes round on surface of water ▸ sometimes the hydrogen catches fire
potassium	violent reaction: ▸ potassium melts and may jump from surface of water ▸ hydrogen immediately catches fire

Alkali metals also react vigorously with **chlorine gas** to make **chlorides**. The chlorides are **colourless crystalline solids**. Again, the reactions get **more vigorous** going down the group.

For example:

lithium + chlorine → lithium chloride

$2Li(s) + Cl_2(g) \rightarrow 2LiCl(s)$

Group 7: the halogens

Name	Symbol of atom	State at room temperature	Colour	Hazards
chlorine	Cl	gas	pale green	☠
bromine	Br	liquid	deep red liquid with red-brown vapour	⚠ and ☠
iodine	I	solid	grey solid with purple vapour	✖

Going down the group, **melting point** and **boiling point** increase.

Halogen molecules are **diatomic** – they are made from two atoms joined together. For example, the formula of bromine is Br_2.

Going **down** group 7, the elements become **less reactive**. For example:

▶ Chlorine reacts so fast with hydrogen that it sometimes explodes.
  Bromine reacts quickly but does not explode.
  Iodine reacts more slowly with hydrogen.

$$\text{chlorine} + \text{hydrogen} \rightarrow \text{hydrogen chloride}$$

▶ Hot iron glows brightly in chlorine gas. It glows less brightly in bromine, and hardly at all in iodine.

$$\text{iron} + \text{chlorine} \rightarrow \text{iron chloride}$$

Halogens are **bleaches**. They also **kill bacteria** in water – this helps prevent the spread of disease.

33

Explaining patterns in the properties of elements

Atomic structure

An atom has a tiny central nucleus made of **protons** and **neutrons**. Around the nucleus are **electrons**.

Particle	Relative mass	Relative charge
proton	1	+1
neutron	1	none
electron	negligible	−1

All atoms of the same element have the same number of protons. For example, every sodium atom has 11 protons. The **proton number** of sodium is 11.

The number of electrons in an atom is the same as the number of protons. Electrons are arranged in **shells**. Each electron shell fills from left to right across a period.

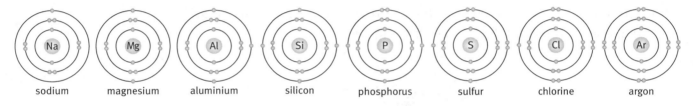

| sodium | magnesium | aluminium | silicon | phosphorus | sulfur | chlorine | argon |

An element's chemical properties depend on its electron arrangement. For example, every group 1 element has one electron in its outer shell. So group 1 elements have similar chemical reactions.

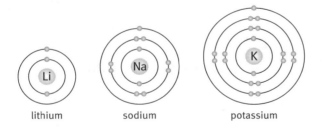

lithium   sodium   potassium

Spectra: evidence for atomic structure

If you hold any lithium compound in a Bunsen flame at the end of a platinum wire, you see a red flame. The compounds of other elements make different colours.

Element	Flame colour
lithium	bright red
sodium	bright yellow
potassium	lilac

When the light from the flame goes through a prism, it makes a **line spectrum**.

Every element has a different spectrum. Chemists have studied these spectra and so discovered new elements, for example helium.

dark blue   pale blue   green   yellow   orange   red

This is the spectrum for helium. The lines are coloured. The series of colours are different for each element.

Ions and ionic compounds

If you melt a compound that is made of a metal joined to a non-metal, it conducts electricity. Charged particles called **ions** carry the current.

An ion is an atom or group of atoms that has gained or lost electrons. So it has an overall charge.

▶ An atom of sodium has 11 positively charged protons in its nucleus. It has 11 negatively charged electrons.

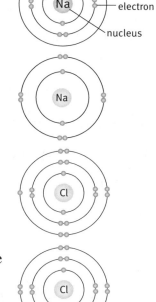

electron

nucleus

A sodium atom loses one electron to become an ion. A sodium ion has 11 protons and 10 electrons. Its overall charge is +1.

▶ A chlorine atom has 17 positively charged protons in its nucleus. It has 17 negatively charged electrons.

A chlorine atom gains one electron to become an ion. A chloride ion has 17 protons and 18 electrons. Its overall charge is −1.

Sodium chloride is a compound that is made from ions. It is **ionic**. Every compound of a group 1 metal with a group 7 metal is ionic.

In solid ionic compounds, the ions are arranged in a regular lattice. So solid ionic compounds form crystals.

When ionic crystals melt or dissolve in water, the ions are free to move independently.

🅗 So ionic compounds conduct electricity when liquid or in solution.

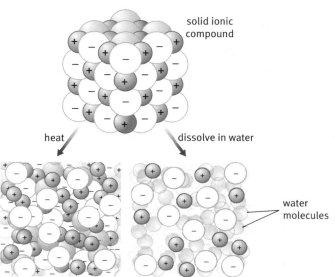

solid ionic compound

heat

dissolve in water

water molecules

⊞ Ion calculations

The formula of sodium chloride (common salt) is NaCl. There is one sodium ion for every chloride ion. The total charge on the ions in the formula is zero. So sodium chloride, like all compounds, is electrically neutral.

	Sodium ion	Chloride ion	Sodium chloride
Charges	+1	−1	(+1) + (−1) = 0

Working out the formulae of an ionic compound
What is the formula of potassium oxide?

The charge on a potassium ion is +1 (K^+).
The charge on an oxide ion is −2 (O^{2-}).
The total charge on the ions in the formula must equal zero.

So potassium oxide has two K^+ ions for every one O^{2-} ion.

So the formula of potassium oxide is K_2O.

Working out the charge on an ion
The formula of calcium bromide is $CaBr_2$.
The charge on one bromide ion is −1.
What is the charge on the calcium ion?

The total charge on the two bromide ions is $-1 \times 2 = -2$.

The total charge on the ions in the formula must be zero (neutral).

So the charge on the calcium ion is +2.

Balancing equations
Balance the equation $HCl + MgO \rightarrow MgCl_2 + H_2O$

▶ Count the number of hydrogen atoms on each side of the arrow.
There are one on the left and two on the right.
Write a big 2 to the left of HCl:

$$2HCl + MgO \rightarrow MgCl_2 + H_2O$$

Now there are two hydrogen atoms on each side.

▶ Count the number of chlorine atoms on each side.
The big 2 to the left of HCl means that there are two on the left.
There are also two on the right of the arrow (in $MgCl_2$).
The number of chlorine atoms is balanced.

▶ Count the number of magnesium atoms on each side of the arrow.
There is one on the left and one on the right.

▶ Count the number of oxygen atoms on each side of the arrow.
There is one on the left and one on the right.

So the balanced equation is: $2HCl + MgO \rightarrow MgCl_2 + H_2O$

Never change the formula of a compound or element to balance an equation.

1 This question is about the elements of group 7 of the periodic table.

a A student writes down information about the properties of group 7 elements. Only some statements are correct.

Put a tick in each of the correct boxes.

Iodine is a grey solid at room temperature. ☐

Bromine is a red-brown gas at room temperature. ☐

Iodine vapour is grey. ☐

Chlorine is a gas at room temperature. ☐

Chlorine is green. ☐ [2]

b Each species of iodine has a different formula.

Complete the table by filling in the empty boxes.

Species	Formula
iodine atom	
iodine molecule	
	I⁻

[3]

c The equations show how sodium reacts with group 7 elements.

i Put a tick in the box next to the most vigorous reaction.

sodium + chlorine → sodium chloride ☐

sodium + fluorine → sodium fluoride ☐

sodium + bromine → sodium bromide ☐

sodium + iodine → sodium iodide ☐ [1]

H

ii Write a balanced symbol equation for the reaction of sodium and fluorine. Include state symbols.

_____ [2]

Total [8]

2 This question is about sodium fluoride.

a A jar of sodium fluoride displays two hazard warning symbols.

i Write the name of the hazard next to each symbol.

 _____

 _____   [2]

ii Suggest one safety precaution a scientist must take when handling sodium fluoride (as well as wearing eye protection).

_____

                                                                          [1]

b i Sodium fluoride consists of sodium and fluoride ions.

The table below shows information about sodium and fluorine atoms and ions.

Complete the table by filling in the empty boxes.

	Number of protons in atom and ion	Number of electrons in atom	Number of electrons in ion	Formula of ion
Sodium	11		10	
Fluorine / fluoride		9		F⁻

                                                                          [2]

ii Complete the diagram below to show the arrangement of electrons in an ion of sodium.   [2]

c Describe what happens to the ions when sodium fluoride dissolves in water.

_____

_____

                                                                          [1]

H **d** A solution of sodium fluoride in pure water conducts electricity.

Use ideas about ions to explain why the solution can conduct electricity.

_____

_____

_____

_____   [2]

e Solid sodium fluoride kills cockroaches and ants.

It is also poisonous to humans.

In 1943 cooks at an American hospital added sodium fluoride to food instead of sodium chloride. Several people died.

Suggest how it was possible for the cooks to make this mistake.

_____

_____

_____   [1]

Total [11]

3 Use the periodic table on page 31 to help you answer this question.

a Give the proton number of silicon. _____   [1]

b Give the symbol of argon. _____   [1]

c Give the name of one element that is in the same group as oxygen.

_____   [1]

d Give the name of one element that is in the same period as magnesium.

_____   [1]

Total [4]

4 This question is about lithium and its compounds.

a A teacher takes a lump of lithium out of a jar of oil.
She cuts off a small piece and adds it to water in a trough.
When the reaction finishes, she adds universal indicator solution to the trough.

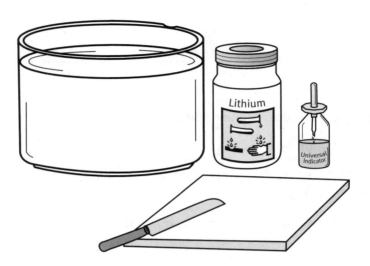

[1]

i A student starts to record his observations.

Complete the table to show what he saw.

What the teacher does	Observations
cuts off a small piece of lithium	shiny when freshly cut then it _____
adds the lithium to water	
adds universal indicator	colour of indicator solution changes from green to _____

[3]

ii Complete the equation for the reaction of lithium with water.

You must balance the equation and give state symbols.

$$Li\ (\underline{})\quad +\quad H_2O\ (\underline{})\quad \rightarrow\quad LiOH\ (\underline{})\quad +\quad H_2\ (\underline{})$$

[2]

b Lithium also reacts with chlorine.

i Give the formula of the product of the reaction. _____ [1]

ii Describe the appearance of the product of the reaction.

_____

[1]

H **c** All the compounds in the table contain the lithium ion, Li^+.

Complete the table by filling in the gaps.

Name of compound	Formula of compound	Formula of non-metal ion
lithium carbonate		CO_3^{2-}
lithium oxide	Li_2O	
lithium _____		Br^-

[4]

Total [12]

5 This question is about the elements of group 1 of the periodic table.

a A student writes down some properties of group 1 elements.

There are three mistakes in the table.

Draw a (ring) around each mistake.

	Melting point (°C)	Formula of hydroxide	Relative reactivity
Lithium	18	LiOH	least reactive element in group 1
Sodium	98	NaOH	more reactive than lithium; less reactive than potassium and caesium
Potassium	64	KOH	more reactive than caesium; less reactive than sodium and lithium
Caesium	28	$Cs(OH)_2$	most reactive element in group 1

b i Predict the formula of the product of the reaction of caesium with chlorine.

_____

[1]

ii A scientist adds caesium to water.

Predict **two** observations he would make.

_____

_____

[2]

iii Predict the names of the products of the reaction of caesium with water.

_____ and _____

[1]

Total [4]

41

6 These diagrams show the electron arrangements in some atoms and ions.

Electron arrangement	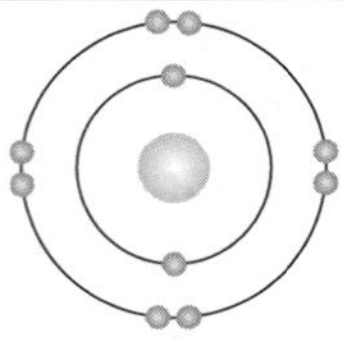	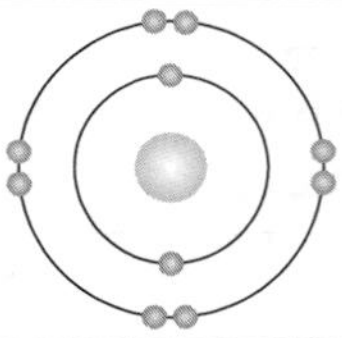	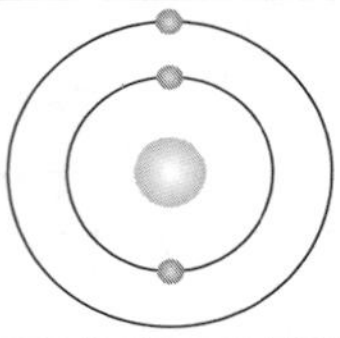	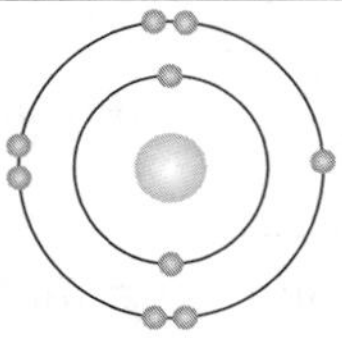
Number of protons in nucleus	9	12	3	9
Letter of atom or ion	A	B	C	D

Using the table, write down the letters of:

a two neutral atoms

_____ and _____   [1]

b a positive ion

_____   [1]

c an atom and an ion of the same element

_____ and _____   [1]

d atoms of two elements in the same period of the periodic table

_____ and _____   [1]

e a negative ion

_____   [1]

H f an atom of an element that has similar properties to sodium

_____   [1]

Total [6]

1   Abdi is standing still.

Write one letter in each box.
Use each letter once, more than once, or not at all.

   a   Which arrow represents the force exerted by the Earth
        on Abdi?

   b   Which arrow represents the force exerted by the floor
        on Abdi?

   c   Which arrow represents the force of gravity?

   d   Which arrow represents the reaction of a surface?

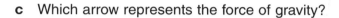

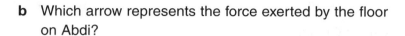

2   Draw and label arrows to show the resultant forces on the rope,
      tricycle, and shopping trolley.

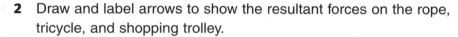

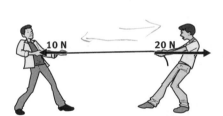

3   Faisal is moving a big loudspeaker.

Which caption belongs where? Write **A**, **B**, or **C** in each box.

   A   The friction force has reached its maximum.

   B   The size of the friction force is less than its maximum.

   C   There is no friction between the loudspeaker and the floor.

I'm pushing really hard,
but it's still not moving!

At last! I've got
it moving!

43

4 David and Ruth are pushing on each other's hands. Neither person is moving.

Write **T** next the statements that are true.
Write **F** next to the statements that are false.

a The size of the force acting on David is less than the size of the force acting on Ruth.

 F

b The size of the force exerted by David is the same as the size of the force acting on Ruth.

 T

c David exerts a bigger force on Ruth than the force that Ruth exerts on David.

 F

d Ruth experiences a bigger force than David.

 F

e Ruth and David exert forces of the same size.

 T

f The force exerted by Ruth is in the same direction as the force exerted by David.

 F

g The forces exerted by David and Ruth are opposite in direction.

T

5 a The statements below explain how the bike starts to move forwards.

They are not in the right order.

A The cyclist pushes down on a pedal.

B The wheels exert a backwards force on the road surface.

C The bike moves forwards.

D The wheels start to turn.

E The other force in the reaction pair is the forward force on the bike.

Fill in the boxes so the parts of the explanation are in a sensible order.

The first one has been done for you.

A D B E C

6 Saima pulls along her suitcase.

The arrows show the directions of the counter-force and the driving force.

Write **T** next to the statements that are true.
Write **F** next to the statements that are false.

a If the driving force is less than the counter-force, the suitcase slows down.

b Saima exerts the driving force to pull the suitcase along.

c If the driving force is equal to the counter-force, the suitcase moves with a constant velocity.

d The counter-force is caused by air resistance only.

e The counter-force is caused by friction and air resistance.

f If the driving force is more than the counter-force, the suitcase speeds up.

g If the driving force is equal to the counter-force, the suitcase cannot move.

7 Calculate the average speed of the following. Include units in your answers.

a A helicopter travels 600 metres in 3 minutes.

Average speed = _____

b A football travels 80 metres in 2 seconds.

Average speed = _____

c A racehorse runs 900 metres in 50 seconds.

Average speed = _____

d A worm moves 32 centimetres in 8 seconds.

Average speed = _____

8 Kelly goes shopping at the mall. On the right is a distance–time graph for part of her time there.

Label the graph by writing one letter in each box.

A Standing still to look at shoes in a shop window

B Walking quickly from the bus stop to the shops

C Walking slowly past some clothes shops

D Running at a constant speed

[H] **E** Starting to run when she realizes she is late to meet her friend

F Slowing down when she sees her friend in the distance

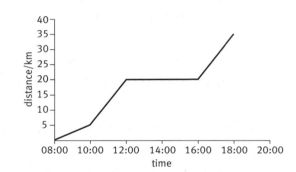

[H] **9** This is a distance–time graph for a whale swimming in the ocean.

a Calculate the whale's average speed between 15:00 hours and 16:00 hours.

Average speed = _____

b Calculate the whale's average speed between 10:00 hours and 12:00 hours.

Average speed = _____

10 a Calculate the momentum in kg m/s of a 2000 kg sports car moving at a velocity of 44 m/s.

Momentum = _____

b Calculate the momentum of a 70 kg person on a 6 kg scooter moving at a velocity of 4 m/s.

Momentum = _____

c Calculate the momentum of a 9 kg baby crawling at a velocity of 1.5 m/s.

Momentum = _____

11 Pawel is a swimmer.

Here is his velocity–time graph for the first 55 m of a 100 m race.

Label the graph by writing one letter in each box.

A Pawel is waiting to dive in. He is stationary.

B Pawel is moving in a straight line. His speed is steadily increasing.

C Pawel has turned round. He has changed direction. His speed is steadily increasing.

D Pawel is moving in a straight line. He is swimming at a constant speed.

E Pawel is turning round. He is stationary for an instant.

F Pawel is moving in a straight line. He is slowing down.

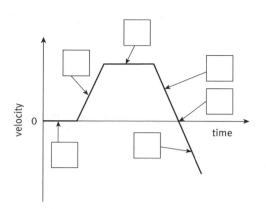

12 A driver does an emergency stop as a child runs out in front of her car.

The car stops in 3 seconds. The resultant force on the car is 5000 N.
Calculate the change in momentum.

Momentum = _____

13 Calculate the kinetic energy of each of the following.

a A 150 kg lion running with a velocity of 20 m/s

Kinetic energy = _____

b A 4000 kg bus moving with a velocity of 25 m/s

Kinetic energy = _____

c A 60 g tennis ball moving with a velocity of 44 m/s

Kinetic energy = _____

14 A monkey drops a banana. Its weight is 1 N. It falls 3 m to the ground.

   a Calculate the change in the banana's gravitational potential energy.

Change in GPE = _____

   b How much kinetic energy does the banana gain?

Kinetic energy = _____

   c What is the speed of the falling banana just before it hits the ground?

Speed = _____

15 Solve the clues to fill in the grid.

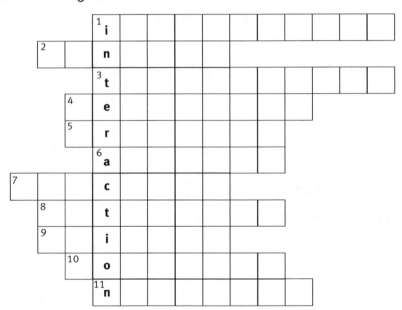

1 The two forces of an _____ pair are equal in size and opposite in direction.

2 A moving object has _____ energy.

3 Lorries and coaches have _____. These are speed–time graphs of the vehicle's motion over 24 hours.

4 Two people pull on a rope in opposite directions. The sum of the forces on the rope, taking direction into account, is the _____ force.

5 The force of _____ arises when you start pushing something over a surface.

6 Calculate the _____ speed of a car by dividing the total distance by the journey time.

7 A floor exerts a _____ force on a table leg that pushes down on it.

8 If you throw a basketball upwards, its gravitational _____ energy increases.

9 The force that makes you move forwards on a scooter is the _____ force.

10 Multiplying the mass of a train by its velocity gives you the train's _____.

11 If a football travels in one direction, its momentum is positive. When it moves in the opposite direction, its momentum is _____.

What are forces?

Interaction pairs

James and Wesley are arm wrestling. No one is winning – their arms are not moving. James's arm *exerts* a force on Wesley's arm. In return, Wesley's arm *exerts* a force on James's arm.

The arrows show the sizes and directions of the forces.

▶ Forces arise from an **interaction** between two objects. They come in pairs.

▶ Each force in an **interaction pair** acts on a different object. The forces are
  – **equal** in size
  – **opposite** in direction

Reaction of surfaces

Latitia is a fire-fighter. She is standing on a roof. Her feet push down on the roof. The roof pushes up on her feet with an equal force. This force is the **reaction of the surface**.

Resultant force

The **resultant force** on an object is the sum of the individual forces that act on it, taking their directions into account.

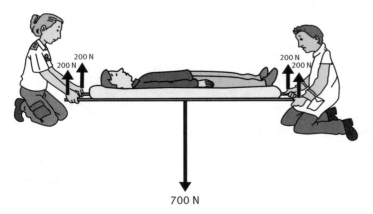

The resultant force on the stretcher is 100 N in an upward direction. So the stretcher starts moving up from the ground.

Friction

David tries to push a small skip that's blocking the road. The force of **friction** stops the skip sliding over the road's surface.

As David pushes harder, the size of the friction force increases. Eventually the friction force reaches its limit. Now the skip moves.

There was no friction force between the skip and the road before David tried to push the skip. Friction arises in response to the force that David applies.

friction = 2500 N

friction = 5000 N

friction at its maximum
(less than 6000 N)

The friction force balances David's push. The skip does not move.

The friction force balances David's push. The skip still does not move.

The skip moves. 6000 N is bigger than the maximum possible friction force for this skip and the road surface.

Getting going

Using friction

When you walk, you push back on the ground with your foot. The friction between your foot and the ground pushes you forward with an equal force.

If the surface is slippery you cannot push back on it, so the ground cannot push you forward.

When a car engine starts, the wheels turn. They exert a big backwards-pushing force on the road surface. The other force in the reaction pair – the forward force – is the same size. This gets the car moving.

If the road is slippery the friction force is small, so the car cannot move forward.

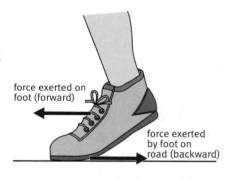

force exerted on foot (forward)

force exerted by foot on road (backward)

Rockets and jet engines

A rocket uses a pair of equal and opposite forces to get moving. It pushes hot burning gases out of its base, so the rocket is pushed in the opposite direction.

A jet engine draws air into its engine and pushes it out at the back. An equal and opposite force pushes the engine forward.

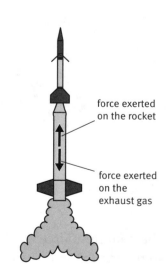

force exerted on the rocket

force exerted on the exhaust gas

Keeping going

Driving and counter-forces

Alex pushes Sam along on a skateboard. Alex exerts the **driving force** to push it forward. There is a counter-force in the opposite direction, because of air resistance and friction.

▶ If the driving force is **greater than** the counter-force, the skateboard speeds up.

▶ If the driving force is **equal** to the counter-force, the skateboard moves at a constant speed in a straight line.

▶ If the driving force is **less than** the counter-force, the skateboard slows down.

The driving force is equal to the counter-force.
The skateboard moves at a constant speed.

Speed and velocity

To calculate the **average speed** of a moving object, use this equation:

$$\textbf{speed (m/s)} = \frac{\textbf{distance travelled (m)}}{\textbf{time taken (s)}}$$

So if a dog runs 20 metres in 10 seconds, its average speed

$$= \frac{20\,\text{m}}{10\,\text{s}}$$

$$= 2\ \text{m/s}$$

Usually, the dog's speed changes as it runs. Its **instantaneous speed** is its speed at a particular instant, or its average speed over a very short time interval. Car speedometers measure instantaneous speed.

The **velocity** of an object is its speed in a certain direction.

Describing motion

Distance–time graphs

Distance–time graphs describe movement.

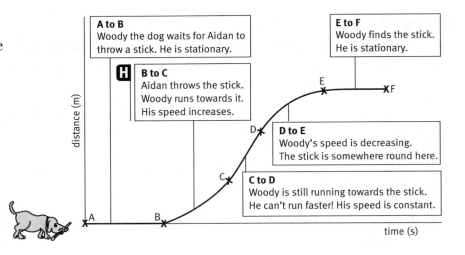

A to B
Woody the dog waits for Aidan to throw a stick. He is stationary.

H B to C
Aidan throws the stick. Woody runs towards it. His speed increases.

E to F
Woody finds the stick. He is stationary.

D to E
Woody's speed is decreasing. The stick is somewhere round here.

C to D
Woody is still running towards the stick. He can't run faster! His speed is constant.

distance (m)

time (s)

H You can use distance–time graphs to **calculate speed**. The steeper the gradient, the higher the speed.

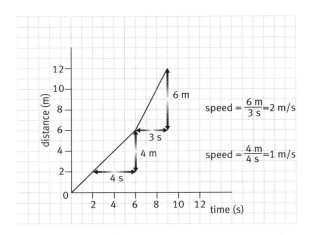

$$\text{speed} = \frac{6\,\text{m}}{3\,\text{s}} = 2\,\text{m/s}$$

$$\text{speed} = \frac{4\,\text{m}}{4\,\text{s}} = 1\,\text{m/s}$$

Velocity–time graphs

Velocity–time graphs show the velocity of a moving object at every instant of its journey. The graph shows the velocity of Ella, an ice dancer.

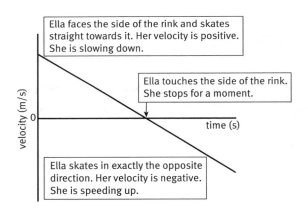

Ella faces the side of the rink and skates straight towards it. Her velocity is positive. She is slowing down.

Ella touches the side of the rink. She stops for a moment.

Ella skates in exactly the opposite direction. Her velocity is negative. She is speeding up.

velocity (m/s)

time (s)

Tachographs

Lorries and coaches have **tachographs** to record their motion.
A tachograph is a **speed–time graph** of a vehicle's motion over 24 hours.

A speed–time graph is similar to a velocity–time graph, but does not show the direction of motion.

The connection between forces and motion

Momentum

All moving objects have **momentum**.

$$\textbf{momentum} \text{ (kg m/s)} = \textbf{mass} \text{ (kg)} \times \textbf{velocity} \text{ (m/s)}$$

For a 0.5 kg bird flying at a velocity of 2 m/s

$$\text{momentum} = 0.5 \text{ kg} \times 2 \text{ m/s}$$
$$= 1 \text{ kg m/s}$$

Momentum depends on direction. We choose a direction to call positive.

When the bird flies in this direction, its momentum is positive.

When the bird flies in the opposite direction, its momentum is negative.

Changing momentum

When a resultant force acts on an object, the momentum of the object changes in the direction of the force:

change of momentum	=	**resultant force**	×	**time for which it acts**
(kg m/s)		(newton, N)		(second, s)

If a 3-second gust of wind from behind the bird exerts a resultant force of 10 N on the bird

$$\text{change of momentum} = 10 \text{ N} \times 3 \text{ s}$$
$$= 30 \text{ kg m/s in the direction the bird is flying}$$

If the resultant force on an object is zero, its momentum does not change.

▶ If it is stationary, it stays still.
▶ If it is already moving, it continues at a steady speed in a straight line.

Road safety measures

If two cars collide, there is a change in momentum. When the cars stop, the momentum decreases to zero.

change of momentum = resultant force × time for which the force acts

Rearranging the equation:

$$\textbf{resultant force} = \frac{\textbf{change in momentum}}{\textbf{time for which the force acts}}$$

So the greater the time for which the force acts, the smaller the resultant force.

Many road safety measures make use of this idea:

▸ Car **crumple zones** squash slowly in a collision. So the collision lasts longer and the resultant force on the car is less.

▸ **Seat belts** stretch in a collision. This makes the change of momentum take longer. So the resultant forces on people in the car are less.

▸ **Air bags** cushion people in a collision. They make the change of momentum take longer. So the resultant force on the person is less.

Describing motion in terms of energy changes

Work done

Barney takes his daughter to the park. He pushes the buggy with a force of 15 N. The force makes the buggy move. Barney is **doing work**.

work done by a force	=	**force**	×	**distance moved by the force**
(joule, J)		(newton, N)		(metre, m)

The park is 500 m away from Barney's house. So

work done by Barney on the buggy = 15 N × 500 m
= 7500 J

Barney **transfers energy** to the buggy. His store of chemical energy decreases.

change in energy = work done
(joule, J)   (joule, J)

change in Barney's store of chemical energy from pushing the buggy = 7500 J

The moving buggy has **kinetic energy**. Kinetic energy depends on **mass** and **velocity**.

kinetic energy = ½ × **mass** × **(velocity)²**
(joule, J) (kilogram, kg) (metre per second, m/s)²

So the faster the buggy moves, and the greater the mass of the child in it, the more kinetic energy it has.

If Barney pushes with a greater force, he does more work and so transfers more energy. The buggy goes faster and its kinetic energy increases.

In fact, the gain of kinetic energy by the buggy is less than the energy transferred from Barney. Barney must also transfer enough energy to overcome air resistance and friction. This energy is lost to the surroundings as heat.

Gravitational potential energy

Catherine picks up her doll from the ground. The doll's **gravitational potential energy (GPE)** increases.

change in GPE = **weight** × **vertical height difference**
(joule, J) (newton, N) (metre, m)

The doll's weight is 3 N. Catherine lifts it 1 m. So

change in doll's GPE = 3 N × 1 m
= 3 J

Catherine drops the doll. It falls 1m to the ground. Its kinetic energy increases.

GPE lost = kinetic energy gained

So the doll gains 3 J of kinetic energy.

To calculate the doll's speed as it falls, use the equation

$$KE = ½ × \textbf{mass} × \textbf{(velocity)}^2$$

Rearranging gives

$$\textbf{velocity} = \sqrt{\frac{2 × \textbf{kinetic energy}}{\textbf{mass}}}$$

$$= \sqrt{\frac{2 × 3\,J}{0.3\,kg}}$$

$$= \sqrt{20\,J/kg}$$

$$= 4.5\,m/s$$

1   A fire engine travels to a fire.

The graph shows its journey.

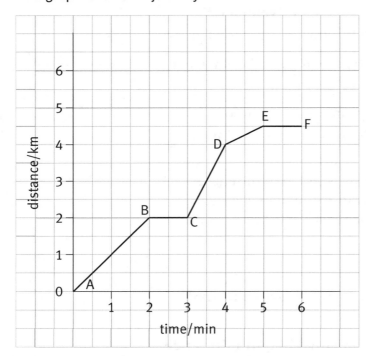

a   **i**   In which part of the journey was the fire engine moving along most slowly?

Draw a (ring) around the correct answer.

A to B   **B to C**   **C to D**   **D to E**   **E to F**   [1]

H

ii   Describe the motion of the fire engine from **B to D**.

It stands still for 1 second + then increasing in speed [2]
by 2k/m by within 1 second.

iii   Calculate the average speed of the fire engine between **A and B**.

Average speed = _____ km/minute   [2]

b   A police car travels to the same fire.

It goes 6000 metres in 500 seconds.

Calculate the average speed of the police car.

$$\frac{6000}{500}$$

Average speed = _____ m/s   [2]

c An ambulance goes along a straight road to get to the fire.

   ▶ For the first 3 minutes its speed increases.
   ▶ For the next 2 minutes it moves at a steady speed.
   ▶ Then it slows down.
   ▶ It stops 7 minutes after its journey began.

Finish the velocity–time graph for the journey.

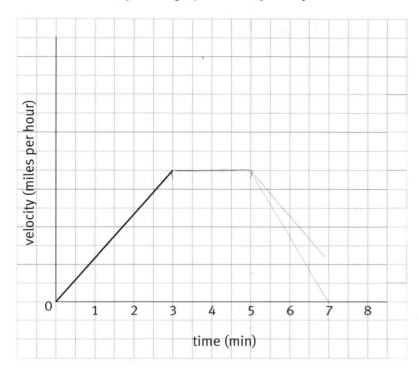

[3]

Total [10]

2   The picture shows a dogsled.

There is a heavy load on the sled.
The dog is trying to pull the sled forward.

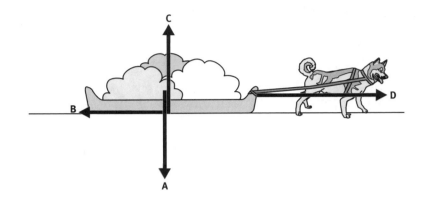

a   Put a tick next to the row which correctly describes the forces on the sled.

A = gravity   **B** = reaction of surface   **C** = friction   **D** = pull of dog   ☐

A = reaction of surface   **B** = friction   **C** = gravity   **D** = pull of dog   ☐

A = gravity   **B** = friction   **C** = reaction of surface   **D** = pull of dog   ☑   [1]

b   A person sits on top of the load on the sled.

What happens to the size of the force exerted by the ground on the sled?

Draw a ⟨ring⟩ around the correct answer.

⟨**increases**⟩   **decreases**   **stays the same**   [1]

c   The dog pulls the sled at a steady speed.

The arrows show some of forces acting on the sled.

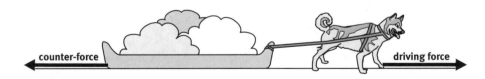

Which statement about these forces is true?

Put a tick in the correct box.

The counter-force is bigger than the driving force.   ☐

The counter-force is smaller than the driving force.   ☐

The counter-force and driving force are equal.   ☑   [1]

Total [3]

3 A penguin stands at the top of a slope. It slides to the bottom.

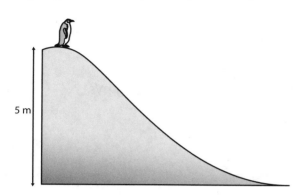

5 m

a i As the penguin slides down the slope its gravitational potential energy (GPE) and its kinetic energy (KE) change.

Tick the statements that are true.

The GPE of the penguin at the top of the slope is less than its GPE at the bottom. ☐

As the penguin slides down the slope, it loses GPE. ☑

The force of gravity does work on the penguin as it slides down the slope. ☑

The penguin's velocity increases as it slides down the slope. ☑

As the penguin slides down the slope, it gains KE. ☑   [2]

ii Calculate the change in the penguin's gravitational potential energy.

The weight of the penguin is 300 N. × 5

Change in GPE = ___1500___ J   [2]

iii Assume that friction is small enough to ignore.

What is the change in the penguin's kinetic energy?

$\frac{1}{2} \times m \times vel.$

Change in KE = _____ J   [1]

b A baby penguin travels down the same slope.

Its mass is 6 kg.

Its velocity at the bottom of the slope is 10 m/s.

Calculate the kinetic energy of the baby penguin at the bottom of the slope.

$\frac{1}{2} \times 6 \times 10^2$

0.5 × 3 ×100

300

KE = ___150___ J   [2]

Total [7]

59

4 A car has a mass of 900 kg. It is moving at 18 m/s.

  a Calculate the momentum of the car.

$$\frac{mo}{m \times v}$$

$$900 \times 18$$

Momentum = _____ kg m/s   [2]

  b The driver is drunk. He crashes the car into a wall.

  The collision lasts 0.01 seconds.

  Calculate the force exerted on the car during the collision.

  Use the equation

  change of momentum = resultant force × time for which it acts

Force = _____ N   [2]

  c The driver was not wearing a seatbelt.

  How do seatbelts help to reduce serious injury?

  Tick the statements that are true.

  Seatbelts stop you moving forward in a crash.   ☐

  Seatbelts stretch during a collision.   ☑

  Seatbelts make the change of momentum of the driver
  happen more quickly.   ☐

  Seatbelts reduce the force that the driver experiences.   ☑

  Seatbelts make you move forward more slowly during
  a collision.   ☐   [2]

Total [6]

5 Jack works in a supermarket. He pushes trolleys back to the shop.

  a Jack pushes the trolleys with a force of 300 N for 150 m.
  Calculate the work done.

$$300 \times 150$$

Answer = _____   [2]

  b What is the change in Jack's store of chemical energy?

Answer = _____   [2]

Total [4]

1 Use words from the box to fill in the gaps.

DNA	**genes**	**chromosomes**	**copied**	**double helix**

Most cells have a nucleus. Inside the nucleus are _____.

These contain _____, which carry information that controls

what an animal or plant is like.

Chromosomes are made from _____ molecules. These molecules are

very long. They are made of two strands twisted together in a spiral,

called a _____. DNA molecules can be

_____ very accurately because of this structure.

2 Look at captions **A** to **H**. Write one letter in each square box on
the diagram.

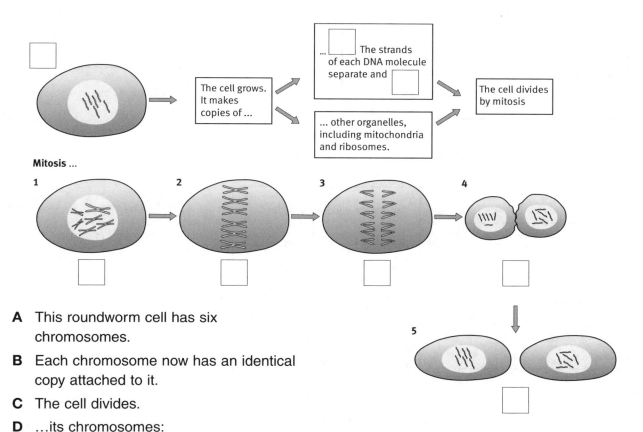

A This roundworm cell has six
chromosomes.

B Each chromosome now has an identical
copy attached to it.

C The cell divides.

D ...its chromosomes:

E There are now two cells. They are each
identical to the parent cell.

F The chromosome copies separate and
move to opposite ends of the cell.

G The chromosomes, with copies attached,
move to the centre of the cell.

H New DNA strands form next to each
strand.

61

3 The flow diagram is about mitosis and meiosis in humans.

Use words and numbers from the box to fill in the gaps.
Use each word or number once, more than once or not at all.

fertilization	eggs	ovaries	testes	sperm	stem	meiosis
mitosis	zygote	2	4	8	16	21	23	42	46

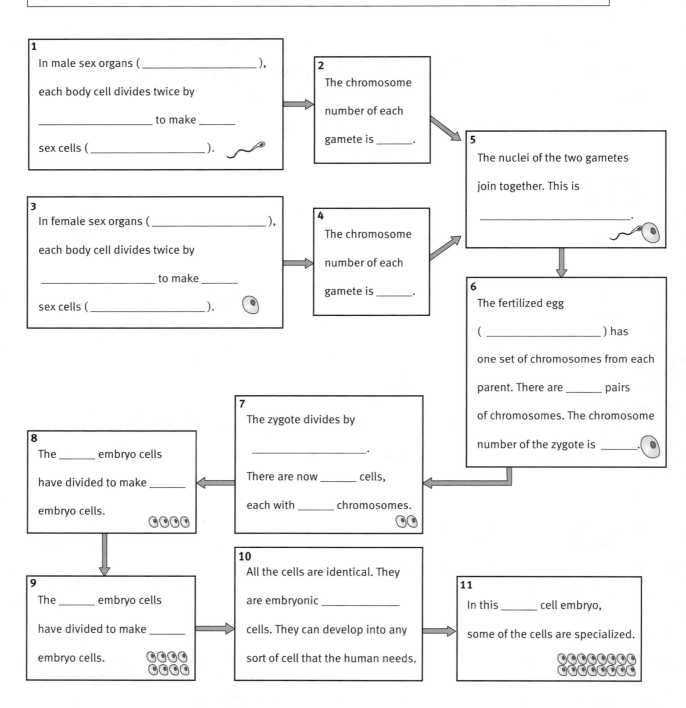

1
In male sex organs (_____),

each body cell divides twice by

_____ to make _____

sex cells (_____).

2
The chromosome

number of each

gamete is _____.

3
In female sex organs (_____),

each body cell divides twice by

_____ to make _____

sex cells (_____).

4
The chromosome

number of each

gamete is _____.

5
The nuclei of the two gametes

join together. This is

_____.

6
The fertilized egg

(_____) has

one set of chromosomes from each

parent. There are _____ pairs

of chromosomes. The chromosome

number of the zygote is _____.

7
The zygote divides by

_____.

There are now _____ cells,

each with _____ chromosomes.

8
The _____ embryo cells

have divided to make _____

embryo cells.

9
The _____ embryo cells

have divided to make _____

embryo cells.

10
All the cells are identical. They

are embryonic _____

cells. They can develop into any

sort of cell that the human needs.

11
In this _____ cell embryo,

some of the cells are specialized.

4 Fill in the empty boxes to show the differences between mitosis and meiosis.

	Meiosis	Mitosis
What does it make?	gametes (sex cells)	
How many new cells does each parent cell make?		2
How many chromosomes are in each new cell?		same as in parent cell
Where does it happen?	in sex organs	
Why does it happen?		so an organism can grow, reproduce and replace damaged cells

5 This activity describes how a DNA molecule makes an exact copy of itself.

▶ In boxes **a** to **d**, draw a (ring) round the correct bold words or numbers.

▶ Draw lines to match each diagram **1** to **4** to the correct description.

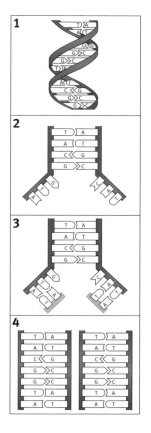

1

2

3

4

a
There are **strong / weak** bonds between the bases.
These bonds break. The DNA opens up from one end
to make **2 / 4 / 6** single strands.

b
There are free bases in the cell. These line up next to
the single strands. Base A pairs with base **T / C**. Base
G pairs with base **T / C**.

c
There are **2 / 4 / 6** different bases in DNA. Base A
always pairs with T. Base G always pairs with base C.
DNA has a double helix shape.

d
The free bases join together to make a second strand.
There are now **2 / 4 / 6** DNA molecules. Each
molecule is made of half old DNA and half new DNA.

6 Complete the speech bubbles to explain how and why stem cells are useful.

So why all this stem cell research?

Well, we reckon they could be really useful for...

Where do stem cells come from?

You can get them from early embryos, umbilical cord blood and adults. Embryonic stem cells are most useful.

Why?

Because...

But isn't that ethically wrong?

Some people think so, yes. Also, embryonic stem cell tissues don't have the same genes as the person getting the transplant. So...

What about therapeutic cloning, then?

Well, there's no problem of rejection here because...

What about adult stem cells? I can't see how that would work. I thought lots of genes are switched off in most cell. So adult stem cells could only grow into a few cell types.

True. If we could switch genes back on, we could use them. But it's really difficult to reactivate genes. The other problem is...

So has there been any success?

Some, we think, yes. We treated 60 patients with heart disease by injecting stem cells from a patient's bone marrow into their heart muscle. This worked better than other potential treatments. We also hope to use stem cell technology to...

7 Write the letters of the statements in sensible places on the Venn diagram.

   A Grow in height and width for their whole lives

   B Contain organs

   C Grow only at meristems

   D Grow all over

   E Contain groups of similar cells called tissues

   F Do not continue to grow for their whole lives

   G Have organs, including leaves, roots and flowers

   H Contain specialized cells

   I Can regrow whole organs if they are damaged

plants   animals

8 Draw lines to link pairs of words.

Write a sentence on each line to show how the two words are linked together.

| unspecialized |

| identical | | stem cells |

| asexual | | cuttings |

| clones | | rooting powder |

| meristem | | auxins |

| roots |

9 All the words in this wordsearch are about the growth and development of plants and animals.

- ▶ Find one word beginning with each of the letters in the table.
- ▶ Write a crossword-type clue for each word.

H	C	D	E	M	O	S	O	B	I	R	T	A	S	C
P	H	O	T	O	T	R	O	P	I	S	M	R	U	E
T	R	U	N	S	P	E	C	I	A	L	I	Z	E	D
I	O	B	A	S	E	S	S	E	U	N	T	T	L	I
S	M	L	H	A	M	E	L	Y	X	R	O	E	C	A
S	O	E	G	P	P	I	L	I	I	H	C	M	U	P
U	S	H	A	E	N	R	A	G	N	B	H	C	N	A
E	O	E	M	B	R	Y	O	N	I	C	O	E	M	Y
G	M	L	E	E	F	E	T	U	S	Y	N	L	R	A
H	E	I	T	T	A	K	D	O	R	A	D	L	W	D
T	N	X	E	E	T	O	G	Y	Z	E	R	S	E	L
J	Y	A	S	M	M	I	N	A	C	T	I	V	E	O
X	S	E	M	A	S	E	L	L	E	N	A	G	R	O

Word	Clue
A	
C	
D	
E	
F	
G	
M	
N	
O	
P	
T	
U	
X	
Y	
Z	

Making new cells

Living things make new cells so that they can grow, reproduce, and replace damaged cells. All new cells are made by **cell division**.

Making new body cells by mitosis

First, a cell grows. It makes copies of its specialized parts (**organelles**), including

▶ chromosomes, which carry genetic information
▶ mitochondria, where respiration takes place

Next, **mitosis** happens. In mitosis the chromosome copies separate and go to opposite ends of the cell. Then the whole cell divides to make two new cells. The new cells are identical to each other and to the parent cell.

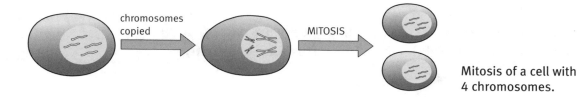

Mitosis of a cell with 4 chromosomes.

Making sex cells by meiosis

Meiosis makes sex cells (**gametes**). It happens in sex organs. In meiosis, a body cell divides twice to make four gametes. Gametes are not identical – they each carry different genetic information.

Gametes have half the number of chromosomes as the parent cell. Human body cells have 46 chromosomes, arranged in 23 pairs. So human gametes (sperm and egg cells) have only 23 single chromosomes.

Meiosis of a cell with 4 chromosomes.

Fertilization

When a human sperm cell fertilizes an egg cell, their nuclei join up. The fertilized egg cell (**zygote**) gets one set of chromosomes from each parent. It has 23 chromosome pairs – 46 chromosomes in all.

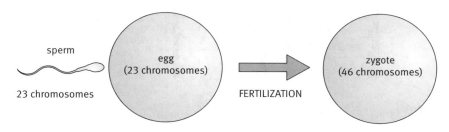

How genes control cell growth and development

DNA and the genetic code

The nucleus of each of your body cells contains enough information to determine the characteristics of your whole body. This information is the **genetic code**.

The genetic code is stored in chromosomes. A chromosome is a very long molecule of **DNA**. A human DNA molecule is made up of about 30 000 genes. Each gene probably contains all the information needed to make a certain protein.

A DNA molecule contains two strands twisted together in a spiral. This is a **double helix**.

▶ Each strand is made of four bases: adenine (A), thymine (T), guanine (G) and cytosine (C).

▶ The bases on the two strands of a DNA molecule always pair up in the same way: A pairs with T and G pairs with C. This is **base pairing**.

Copying DNA

When a cell grows, it makes copies of its chromosomes. Base pairing in DNA means that the copies are exact. The copies are made like this:

▶ Bonds between the bases split. So the two strands separate.
▶ The cell contains free bases. These start to make new strands.
▶ G always pairs with C, and A always pairs with T.
   So the two new strands are identical to the original strands.

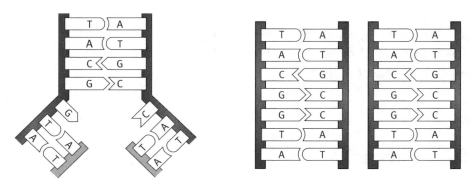

One DNA strand...   ...makes...   ...two new DNA strands

Making proteins

Cells make proteins from about 20 **amino acids**. There are thousands of different proteins. Each protein has a certain combination of amino acids joined together in a particular order.

H The order of bases in a gene is the code for joining amino acids in the correct order to make a particular protein. Each amino acid has a three-base code (a **triplet code**). So four bases can code for all 20 amino acids.

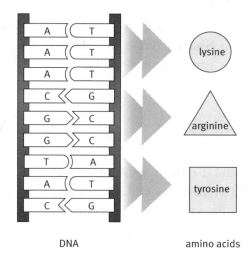

DNA   amino acids

The genetic code for making proteins is held on DNA in the cell nucleus. But proteins are made in ribosomes in the cell cytoplasm. Genes cannot leave the nucleus. So messenger RNA (**mRNA**) molecules transfer the genetic code from the nucleus to ribosomes. mRNA molecules are smaller than DNA, so they can fit through gaps in the membrane round the nucleus.

H mRNA differs from DNA in that it has just one strand and the base U replaces base T in DNA.

This is how a protein is made:

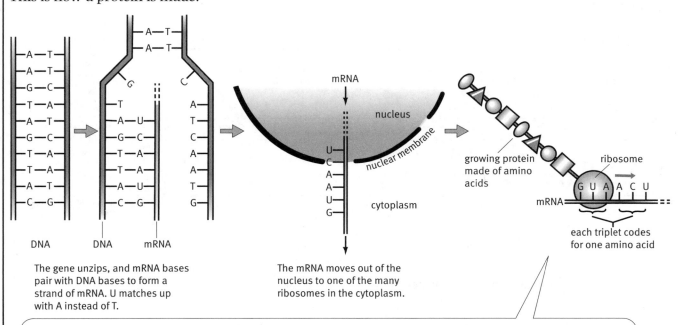

DNA   DNA   mRNA

The gene unzips, and mRNA bases pair with DNA bases to form a strand of mRNA. U matches up with A instead of T.

The mRNA moves out of the nucleus to one of the many ribosomes in the cytoplasm.

each triplet codes for one amino acid

The ribosome attaches to one end of the mRNA. As it moves along the mRNA, the ribosome reads the genetic code so that it can join the amino acids together in the correct order. When it has finished, the ribosome releases the protein into the cytoplasm and starts to make another one.

From single cell to whole organism

Embryo development

A fertilized egg cell (zygote) divides by mitosis to make an embryo.

Up to the eight-cell stage of a human embryo, every cell is identical. Each cell can develop into any sort of cell that the organism needs – or even a whole organism. These are **embryonic stem cells**.

After the eight-cell stage, the embryo's cells become specialized. They have a particular structure to do a particular job. Specialized cells of the same type group together to form **tissues**. For example, muscle cells group together to make muscle tissue.

Gene switching

The nucleus of each of your body cells contains an exact copy of the DNA of the original zygote. So every cell contains the same genes – about 30 000 of them. But not all these genes are active in every cell. Each cell makes only the proteins it needs to be a particular type of cell. So genes that give instructions to make other proteins are not active; they are **switched off**.

For example, hair cells make keratin. So the genes for the enzymes that make keratin are switched on. Hair cells do not make muscle. So the genes for the enzymes that make muscle are switched off.

Salivary gland cells make amylase. So the genes for the enzymes that make amylase are switched on. The genes for the enzymes that make keratin and muscle are switched off.

All cells respire, so the genes needed for respiration are switched on in all cells.

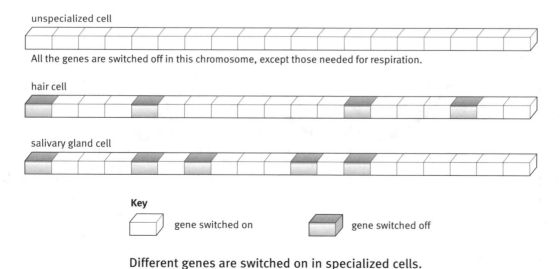

unspecialized cell

All the genes are switched off in this chromosome, except those needed for respiration.

hair cell

salivary gland cell

Key

☐ gene switched on   ▨ gene switched off

Different genes are switched on in specialized cells.

⊞ Stem cell technology

Stem cells are unspecialized cells. They can divide and develop into specialized cells. Stem cells come from early embryos, umbilical cord blood, and adults.

Scientists hope to use stem cells to treat diseases and replace damaged tissues. For example, skin cells grown from stem cells could be used to treat burns. Nerve cells grown from stem cells could treat spinal injuries.

There are problems with stem cell technology.

▶ Embryonic stem cells are most useful, as all their genes are still switched on. But . . .
 – some people have ethical objections to using them
 – tissues grown from embryonic stem cells have different genes to the patients receiving the tissue. So patients must take drugs to stop their bodies rejecting the transplanted tissue.

▶ Adult stem cells have most of their genes switched off. So they can grow into only a few cell types.

Therapeutic cloning switches on inactive genes in adult body cell nuclei. It also overcomes the problem of patients rejecting transplanted tissue.

This is how to produce an organ or tissue needed by a patient:

▶ Take a nucleus out of a human egg cell. Replace it with a nucleus from a body cell of the patient.

▶ The egg cell makes an embryo. Its genes are the same as the patient's genes.

▶ After 5 days, put stem cells from the embryo in a dish of nutrients.

▶ The stem cells can develop into different organs and tissues.

▶ Transplant the organ or tissue required into the patient.

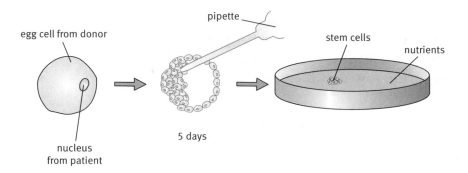

egg cell from donor
pipette
stem cells
nutrients
nucleus from patient
5 days

How plants grow and develop

Cells, tissues, and organs

Most plant cells are specialized. They group together in tissues. Groups of tissues organize themselves into organs, for example leaves, flowers, and roots.

Some plant cells remain unspecialized. These **meristem cells** can develop into any type of specialized plant cell. So plants can regrow whole organs if they are damaged.

Growth

Most plants grow throughout their lives. They grow when meristem cells divide to make new cells.

▶ Meristem cells in shoot tips divide to make stems taller.
▶ Meristem cells in root tips divide to make roots longer.
▶ Rings of meristem cells in stems and roots divide to make them wider.

Plants tend to grow towards the light. This is **phototropism**. Plants need light to photosynthesize. So phototropism increases a plant's chance of survival.

Phototropism involves plant hormones called **auxins**.

If light is above a growing shoot, auxins spread out evenly. The shoot grows straight up.

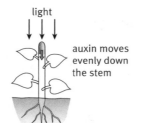

light

auxin moves evenly down the stem

If light comes from the side, auxins move to the shady side. Auxins make cells on the shady side grow faster. So the shoot bends towards the light.

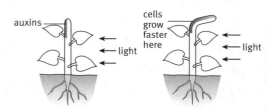

auxins

light

cells grow faster here

light

Cuttings

Gardeners sometimes grow plants that are genetically identical to a parent plant. They do this by taking **cuttings**. The new plant and the parent plant are **clones**.

First, the gardener chooses a plant with features that he wants. Then he cuts a shoot or leaf from the plant. This is a cutting. The gardener puts the cutting in water, compost or **rooting powder**. Rooting powder contains auxins.

The shoot's meristem cells divide to make new cells. Auxins encourage some of these cells to develop into root cells. Other unspecialized cells become

▶ other organs, for example flower or leaves
▶ tissues, for example xylem, which transports water, and phloem, which transports sugar.

1 Giraffes have 30 chromosomes in each body cell.

  a Finish the sentences by choosing the best words and numbers from the box.

  Use each word or number once, more than once, or not at all.

gametes	zygotes	different		ovaries		testes	
penis	identical	1	2	4	15	30	60

  Giraffes make sex cells by meiosis. Sex cells are also called

  ___gametes___. In male giraffes, meiosis happens in the

  ___~~ovaries~~ testes___. In meiosis, one body cell divides to make _~~4~~ 2_ sex

  cells. Each of these cells carries ___different___ genetic information.

  There are _~~2~~ 15_ chromosomes in one giraffe sex cell.   [5]

  b After sexual intercourse, the nucleus of a male sex cell joins to the nucleus of a female sex cell.

  i Give the name of the female sex cell.

  ___~~ovaries~~ ovum___   [1]

  ii Give the name of the process in which the nucleus of a male sex cell joins to the nucleus of a female sex cell.

  ___fertilisation___   [1]

  c The steps below describe how body cells grow and divide in giraffe embryos.
  They are in the wrong order.

  A The chromosome copies separate and go to opposite ends of the cell.

  B These are identical to each other and to the parent cell.

  C The cell makes copies of its specialised parts, including the chromosomes.

  D The cell divides to make two new cells.

  Fill in the boxes to show the correct order.   [3]

  C   A   D   B

  Total [10]

2 James has a rose plant.

He cuts a piece of stem from the plant. This is a cutting.

He puts the cutting in rooting powder.

The cutting grows roots.

A new rose plant grows.

a **i** Why do gardeners take cuttings?

Tick the **two best** reasons.

They can grow many new plants quickly and cheaply. ☐

They can grow many new plants with different features
by taking cuttings from just one plant. ☐

Plants grown from cuttings are more resistant to disease
than plants grown from seed. ☑

They can reproduce a plant with exactly the features
they want. ☑

Plants grown from cuttings are stronger than plants
grown from seed ☐ [1]

ii Give the name of the plant hormone in rooting
powder.

auxins [1]

iii Name the unspecialized plant cells that divide to make
root cells in cuttings.

_____ [1]

iv Name two other plant organs (not roots) that are made by the
division of unspecialized plant cells in cuttings.

leaves

_____ [2]

b The shoot of the rose plant grows towards the light.

   i Explain how growing towards the light helps the plant to survive.

   because light is needed for the plant to photosynthesise.

   [1]

   ii Give the scientific name for the process in which growing plant shoots bend towards the light.

   photohropism

   [1]

   iii The drawing shows the shoot of a rose plant. The arrows show the direction of the light.

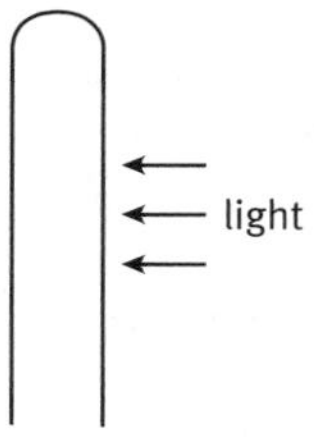

   ← light

   In which drawing below does the shaded area show where the concentration of plant hormones is greatest?

   Draw a (ring) around the correct answer.

   A   B   C   D   [1]

   Total [8]

3 A company sells 'stem cell gift certificates'.

When a baby is born, a nurse takes blood from the baby's umbilical cord. The company separates stem cells from the blood. It stores the stem cells at −180 °C for 25 years.

a **i** What are stem cells?

Put a tick next to the **best** definition.

Stem cells are unspecialized cells. They join together to make specialized cells. ☐

Stem cells are unspecialized cells. They divide and develop into specialized cells. ☑

Stem cells are specialized cells. They divide and develop into unspecialized cells. ☐

Stem cells are specialized cells. They join together to make unspecialized cells. ☐ [1]

ii The company says that doctors can use the stem cells to treat illnesses the baby may get in future.

How might doctors use the stem cells to treat heart disease?

Put a tick next to the **most likely** answer.

They will make a heart disease vaccine from the stem cells. ☐

They will grow heart muscle cells from the stem cells. ☐

They will make a heart disease medicine from the stem cells. ☐

They will inject stem cells into the patient's bloodstream. ☐ [1]

b One source of stem cells is umbilical cord blood.

i Name **one other** source of stem cells.

_____ [1]

ii Give one **problem** of using stem cells from this source to treat disease or replace damaged tissues.

_____

_____ [1]

iii Read this leaflet. It is written by people who think that umbilical cord stem cells should not be taken and stored.

Warning to women about to give birth

Do you have a stem cell gift certificate? We suggest you don't use it.

Scientists hope umbilical cord stem cells will cure many diseases in future. But so far these stem cells have cured only very few diseases. It is unlikely that your child will get one of these diseases.

Taking blood from the umbilical cord is not easy. It will distract midwives when they should be concentrating on making sure that the mother and baby are safe and well.

We also don't know how long stem cells can be stored for.

Why might doctors give pregnant women this warning?

Put a tick next to the **three best** answers.

Taking blood from the umbilical cord could harm the mother or baby. ☐

Umbilical cord stem cells can produce red blood cells only. ☐

So far, there has only been little success in using stem cells to treat disease. ☐

There is only a small risk of getting diseases that stem cells could treat. ☐

Umbilical cord stem cells can produce white blood cells only. ☐

[3]

Total [7]

4 **a** The picture shows part of a DNA molecule.

A DNA molecule contains two strands twisted together in a spiral.

Give the name of the structure.

_____ [1]

H **b** Human DNA molecules contain up to 30 000 genes.

What does a gene do?

Tick the correct answer.

It gives instructions for joining amino acids in the correct order to make a certain base. ☐

It gives instructions for joining bases in the correct order to make a certain amino acid. ☐

It gives instructions for joining bases in the correct order to make a certain protein. ☐

It gives instructions for joining amino acids in the correct order to make a certain protein. ☐ [1]

c The steps below describe how a DNA molecule makes an exact copy of itself.

They are in the wrong order.

A The DNA molecule opens up from one end and makes two single strands.

B Bonds between base pairs break.

C The free bases join together to make two new strands.

D Free bases in the cell line up next to the single strands.

Fill in the boxes to show the correct order.

☐ ☐ ☐ ☐ [3]

Total [5]

1 Look at the diagram below and complete the boxes like this:

▶ Write the letters A, B, C, and D in the correct small squares.

   A a mixture of elements and compounds with small molecules

   B a mixture of water and ionic compounds

   C a mixture of minerals

   D contain long chain molecules based on carbon

▶ Write the names of up to four elements or compounds in each box.
   Choose from this list:

oxygen	glucose	sodium chloride	silicon dioxide
argon	DNA	potassium bromide	carbon dioxide
nitrogen		magnesium chloride	aluminium oxide

2 Make up 12 sentences using the phrases in the table.

Each sentence must include a phrase from each column.

Write your answers in the grid at the bottom.

For example, the sentence:

> Carbon dioxide… never conducts electricity… because… no ions or electrons can move freely to carry the current

is

A	i	10

A Carbon dioxide	**a** has a high melting point	because	1	the forces of attraction between the molecules are weak
	b has a low melting point		2	the atoms are held by strong covalent bonds in a giant structure
	c has a high boiling point		3	it takes a lot of energy to separate its ions to make a gas
B Silicon dioxide	**d** has a low boiling point		4	there are strong attractive forces between its oppositely charged ions
	e conducts electricity when it is liquid or dissolved in water		H 5	there are strong bonds between its positive ions and a 'sea' of negative electrons
			6	its ions are free to move independently
C Sodium chloride	**f** makes crystals		7	its layers of atoms can move over each other
	g is malleable		8	its oppositely charged ions are held together in a three-dimensional pattern
	h is very hard		9	much energy is needed to break the strong bonds between the atoms
D Copper	**i** never conducts electricity		10	no ions or electrons can move freely to carry the current

A	i	10

3 Draw lines to match each formula to a diagram.

CO_2

H_2O

O_2

Ar

4 Draw lines to match each substance with its type of structure and its melting point. One has been done for you.

Substance
nitrogen gas
silicon dioxide
sodium chloride
glucose

Type of structure
giant covalent
giant ionic
simple covalent
simple covalent

Melting point (°C)
1610
−210
about 150
801

H 5 Use the information in the table to work out the formulae of the compounds below.

Positive ions	Negative ions
Na^+	Cl^-
Mg^{2+}	Br^-
K^+	$SO_4{}^{2-}$

a Sodium chloride _____

b Magnesium chloride _____

c Potassium bromide _____

d Magnesium sulfate _____

6 Use the data in the table to answer the questions.

Element	% by mass of this element in the lithosphere	% by volume of this element in the atmosphere
aluminium	8	0
argon	0	1
iron	5	0
nitrogen	0	78
oxygen	47	21
silicon	28	0

a Name the most abundant element in the lithosphere. _____

b Name the most abundant element in the atmosphere. _____

c Name the element that is abundant in both the lithosphere and the atmosphere.

_____

d Name the most abundant non-metal in the lithosphere. _____

e Name the most abundant metal in the lithosphere. _____

7 Edward and Mary are buying an engagement ring.

Finish their conversation.

8 Proteins are polymers. They are built by joining together amino acid monomers.

The table shows the structural formulae of four amino acids.

Write their molecular formulae in the empty boxes. One has been done for you.

Structural formula	Molecular formula
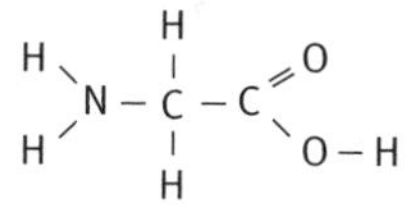	$C_2H_5O_2N$
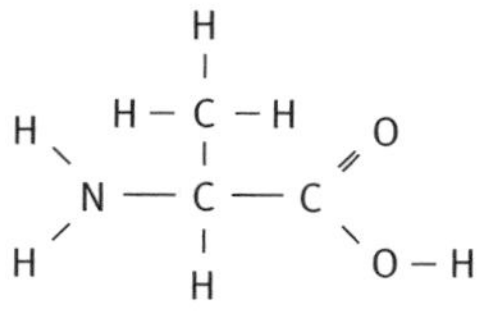	
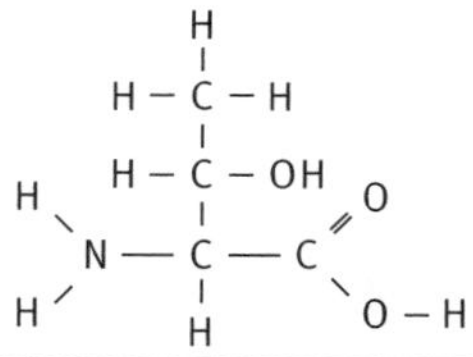	
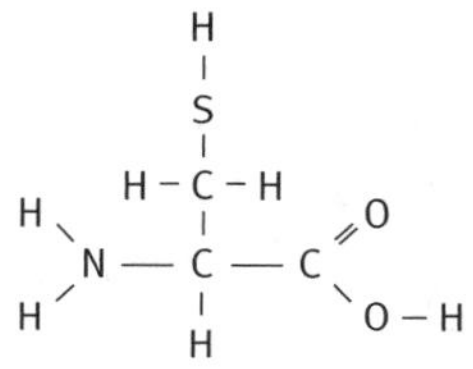	

9 Balance each equation. Then

▶ draw a (ring) in **red** round the substance that is reduced

▶ draw a (ring) in **blue** round the substance that is oxidized

a $ZnO(s)$ $+$ $C(s)$ $\rightarrow$ $Zn(s)$ $+$ $CO(g)$

b $Fe_2O_3(s)$ $+$ $C(s)$ $\rightarrow$ $Fe(s)$ $+$ $CO(g)$

H **10** Use the periodic table on page 31 to help you answer these questions.

a Calculate the mass of zinc in 162 tonnes of zinc oxide, ZnO.

Answer = _____

b Calculate the mass of aluminium in 51 kg of aluminium oxide, Al_2O_3.

Answer = _____

11 The stages below describe how aluminium is extracted from bauxite ore.

They are in the wrong order.

A Add sodium hydroxide solution to remove impurities from the bauxite.

B Pass an electric current through the aluminium oxide.

C Melt the aluminium oxide.

D Collect liquid aluminium from the tapping hole at the bottom of the tank.

E Aluminium forms at the negative electrode and oxygen forms at the positive electrode. The oxygen then reacts with the carbon electrodes to give off carbon dioxide gas.)

Fill in the boxes to show the correct order. The first one has been done for you.

12 Write the answers to the clues in the spiral.

The first letter of each answer is the last letter of the one before it.

1 The chemical that carries genetic information in cells.

2 The most abundant metal in the lithosphere.

3 A naturally occurring element or compound in the lithosphere is called a _____.

4 The rigid outer layer of the Earth.

5 Aluminium is extracted from bauxite by _____.

6 The hydrosphere is a mixture of water and dissolved _____.

7 Silicon dioxide exists as quartz and _____.

8 There are _____ forces of attraction between oppositely charged ions in ionic compounds.

9 The most abundant element in the biosphere is _____.

10 The most abundant element in the atmosphere is _____.

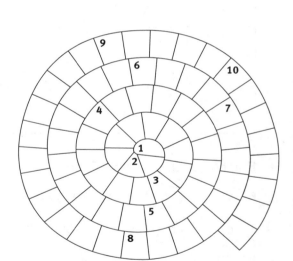

The chemicals of the atmosphere

Dry air is a mixture of gases. Some of the gases are elements; the others are compounds.

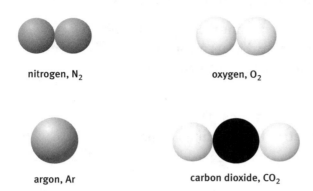

nitrogen, N_2

oxygen, O_2

argon, Ar

carbon dioxide, CO_2

The elements and compounds of the air are made of small molecules. There are weak forces of attraction between the molecules. So the elements and compounds have low melting points and boiling points. They are gases.

H The atoms in a molecule share electrons. The electrostatic attraction between positively charged nuclei and negatively charged electrons is very strong. So the **covalent bonds** between the atoms within a molecule are very strong.

Pure molecular compounds cannot conduct electricity. This is because their molecules are not charged.

The chemicals of the hydrosphere

Sea water is a mixture of water and dissolved **ionic compounds**, called **salts**.

Ionic compounds contain positive and negative ions. In ionic **solids**, the ions are arranged in a **giant three-dimensional pattern** to make **crystals**. There are very strong attractive forces between the oppositely charged ions. This is ionic bonding.

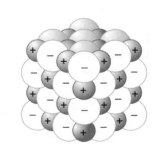

Ionic compounds have **high melting points**. This is because much energy is needed to break down a solid's giant structure of ions. They also have **high boiling points** – it takes a lot of energy to separate a liquid's ions to make a gas.

When an ionic crystal dissolves in water, its ions are free to move independently. This is why solutions of ionic compounds conduct electricity.

H You can work out the formula of an ionic compound if you know the charges on its ions. Page 36 shows how to do this.

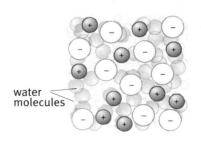

water molecules

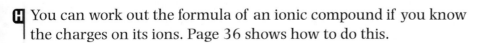

The chemicals of the lithosphere

The **lithosphere** is the Earth's rigid outer layer. It consists of the **crust** and the **part of the mantle** just below the crust. It is made of a **mixture of minerals**. Minerals are compounds that occur naturally.

Silicon, oxygen, and aluminium are the most common elements in the Earth's crust. Much of the silicon and oxygen exists as a compound, **silicon dioxide**. Silicon dioxide is the main mineral of **sandstone**. It also exists as **quartz** in granite.

Solid silicon dioxide has a **giant structure** of atoms. The atoms are held together by **strong covalent bonds**. Its structure explains its properties.

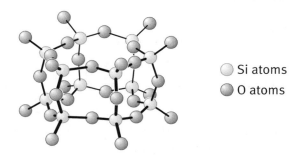

○ Si atoms
◉ O atoms

A small part of a crystal of quartz

Property	Explanation
high melting point	Much energy is needed to break the strong covalent bonds in the giant structure of atoms.
high boiling point	
very hard	Much energy is needed to break the strong covalent bonds between atoms on the surface.
insoluble in water	Much energy is needed to break the strong covalent bonds between the atoms.
does not conduct electricity	It contains no charged particles to move freely and carry the current.

Quartz is the main mineral in several **gemstones**, such as amethyst. Amethyst contains traces of manganese and iron oxides. These give the mineral its violet colour. Valuable gemstones are beautiful, rare, and hard.

The chemicals of the biosphere

The **biosphere** is all living things. Living things are based on the element **carbon**.

Carbon makes a huge variety of compounds because its atoms can form long chains, rings, and other complex structures.

▸ Atoms of **hydrogen, oxygen**, and **nitrogen**, with small amounts of other elements, join to carbon chains to make proteins and DNA.
▸ Carbohydrates consist of carbon, hydrogen, and oxygen.

Carbohydrates, proteins, and DNA are **molecular**. For example:

Name of compound	Diagram	Elements present	Formula
cysteine, a component of proteins		carbon, hydrogen, oxygen, nitrogen, sulfur	$C_3H_7O_2SN$
glucose, a carbohydrate		carbon, hydrogen, oxygen	$C_6H_{12}O_6$
DNA	Part of DNA molecule	carbon, hydrogen, oxygen, nitrogen, phosphorus	

How chemicals move between the 'spheres'

Elements move between the biosphere, atmosphere, lithosphere, and hydrosphere when living things grow, die, and decay.

The **carbon cycle** flow chart shows some of the **chemical changes** that happen as carbon moves between the spheres.

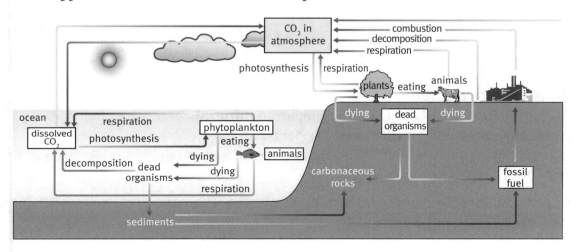

Metals

Using metals

Metals have many uses. Their uses depend on their properties.

Metals are **malleable** – they bend without breaking.

Metals are **strong**.

Metals **conduct electricity**.

Metals have **high melting points**.

Explaining metals' properties

Solid metals have giant crystalline structures. Strong **metallic bonds** hold the atoms together. This explains why metals are strong and why they have high melting points.

Metallic bonds are **flexible**, so layers of atoms can slide over each other. This is why metals are malleable.

Ⓗ Metal atoms easily lose their outermost electrons to make positive ions. The electrons move freely between the ions. Electrostatic forces between the positive ions and the sea of negative electrons hold the structure together.

The sea of electrons explains why metals conduct electricity well. When a metal wire conducts electricity, free electrons drift from one end of the wire towards the other.

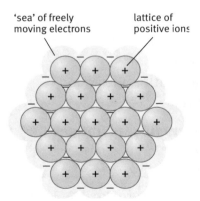

'sea' of freely moving electrons

lattice of positive ions

A model of metallic bonding

Extracting metals from minerals

In the lithosphere, most metals are joined to other elements in **minerals**. Rocks that contain useful minerals are called **ores**. Copper is extracted from the mineral copper iron sulfide ($CuFeS_2$). The ore that contains this mineral is copper pyrites.

Ores contain different amounts of minerals. Often, a huge amount of ore contains only a tiny mass of a useful mineral.

H You can calculate the mass of a metal in a mineral. For example:

What is the mass of aluminium in 100 kg of aluminium oxide, Al_2O_3?

▶ Use the periodic table on page 31 to find out the relative atomic masses of the elements in the mineral.
Al = 27   O = 16

▶ Calculate the mineral's relative formula mass
$(27 \times 2) + (16 \times 3) = 102$

▶ Calculate the relative mass of the metal in the formula
$27 \times 2 = 54$

▶ Calculate the mass of metal in 1 kg of the mineral
54 kg ÷ 102 kg = 0.53 kg

▶ Multiply by 100 to find the mass of metal in 100 kg of the mineral
0.53 kg × 100 = 53 kg

The method used to extract a metal from its ore depends on the metal's reactivity.

Metal	Method
potassium sodium calcium magnesium aluminium	electrolysis of molten ores
zinc iron tin lead	reduction of ores using carbon
silver gold	metals occur uncombined

MORE REACTIVE ⬆ LESS REACTIVE

Extracting metals by heating with carbon
Iron, copper, and zinc are extracted from their oxides by heating with carbon. For example:

zinc oxide	+	carbon	→	zinc	+	carbon monoxide
ZnO(s)	+	C(s)	→	Zn(s)	+	CO(g)

Zinc oxide loses oxygen. It is **reduced**. Carbon gains oxygen. It is **oxidized**.

Extracting metals by electrolysis
Metals near the top of the reactivity series, like aluminium, are joined very strongly to other elements in their minerals. They cannot be extracted by heating with carbon. So they are extracted by **electrolysis**.

Aluminium oxide is an ionic compound. When it melts, its ions can move independently. So liquid aluminium oxide conducts electricity. It is an **electrolyte**. Electrolytes break down, or **decompose**, when an electric current passes through them. This is electrolysis.

To extract aluminium from aluminium oxide:

1 Add sodium hydroxide to remove impurities. Pure aluminium oxide remains.

2 Melt the pure aluminium oxide. Pour it into this equipment:

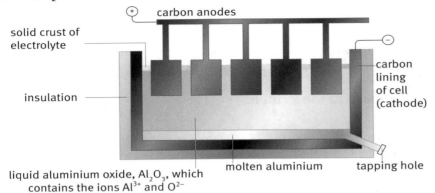

solid crust of electrolyte

carbon anodes

insulation

carbon lining of cell (cathode)

liquid aluminium oxide, Al_2O_3, which contains the ions Al^{3+} and O^{2-}

molten aluminium

tapping hole

3 Pass an electric current through the electrolyte

▶ Aluminium (a metal) forms at the negative electrode (cathode). Al^{3+} ions gain electrons from the electrode to make neutral aluminium atoms:

$$Al^{3+} + 3e^- \rightarrow Al$$

▶ Oxygen (a non-metal) forms at the positive electrode (anode). O^{2-} ions give electrons to the positive electrode to make neutral oxygen atoms:

$$O^{2-} \rightarrow O + 2e^-$$

Oxygen atoms then join together to make oxygen molecules:

$$O + O \rightarrow O_2$$

Environmental impacts of using metals

1 Living things contain carbohydrates and proteins.

a What type of structure do carbohydrates have?

Tick the correct box.

giant ionic ☐

metallic ☐

molecular ☐

giant covalent ☐ [1]

b Glucose is a carbohydrate.

The table shows the percentage by mass of the elements in glucose.

Element	Percentage by mass
carbon	40
hydrogen	7
oxygen	53

Calculate the mass of carbon in 200 g of glucose.

Answer = _____ g [2]

c Proteins are made from amino acids.

Serine is an amino acid.

The diagram shows the structure of a serine molecule.

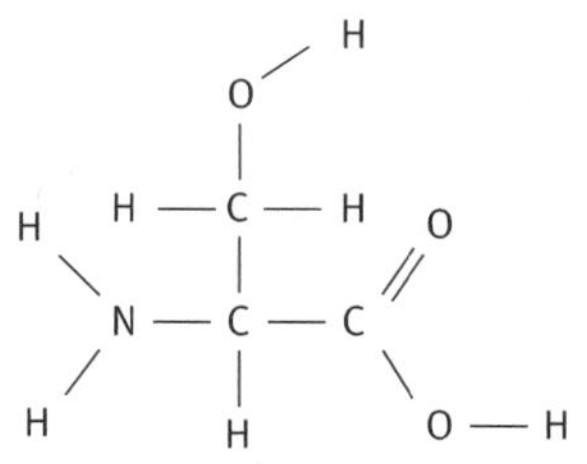

i Write the names of the four elements in serine.

_____ [1]

ii Complete the formula of serine.

C_3———— [1]

Total [5]

2 The diagram shows part of the oxygen cycle.

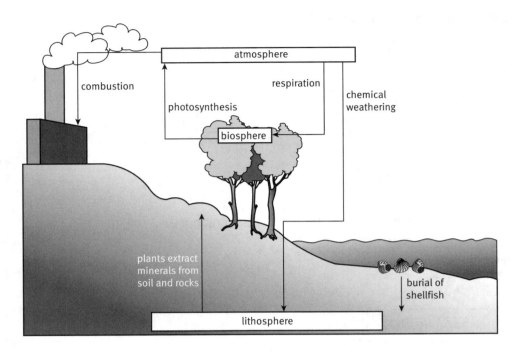

a i Give the names of two processes which add oxygen to the atmosphere.

_____ and _____ [1]

ii Describe two ways in which oxygen is added to the lithosphere.

_____

_____

_____

_____ [2]

b Oxygen gas in the atmosphere is made of small molecules.

   i Give the formula of an oxygen molecule. _____ [1]

   ii Which properties are typical of substances that are made of small molecules?

     Tick the correct boxes.

     They have low melting points ☐

     They have high boiling points ☐

     They do not conduct electricity ☐

     They have high densities ☐ [2]

c Olivine is a rock. Its formula is Fe_2SiO_4.

Chemical weathering of olivine removes oxygen from the atmosphere.

The weathering reaction makes haematite, Fe_2O_3.

   i Finish balancing the equation for the weathering reaction.

     $2Fe_2SiO_4 + 4H_2O + O_2 \rightarrow$ ___ $Fe_2O_3 +$ ___ H_4SiO_4 [2]

   ii Iron metal is extracted from haematite.

     Calculate the mass of iron that can be extracted from 320 kg of haematite.

     Answer = _____ kg [2]

Total [10]

3 a Magnesium bromide is an ionic compound.

It used to be used as a sedative. It is also a laxative.

i In which 'sphere' are many ionic compounds found dissolved in water?

Tick one box.

Lithosphere ☐

Atmosphere ☐

Hydrosphere ☐ [1]

ii Draw lines to match each property of magnesium bromide with a reason.

Property
When solid, it does not conduct electricity.
It has a high melting point.
When solid, it forms crystals.
When liquid, it conducts electricity.

Reason
There are very strong attractive forces between the positive and negative ions.
The ions are arranged in a regular pattern.
The charged particles cannot move.
The charged particles can move independently.

[3]

H

iii Magnesium bromide contains these ions:

Mg^{2+} and Br^-

What is the formula of magnesium bromide? _____ [2]

b In World War Two, magnesium was extracted from seawater to make bombs.

The mass of magnesium ions in 1 m³ of seawater is 1.3 kg.

Calculate the volume of seawater that contains 100 kg of magnesium ions.

Answer = _____ [2]

c i Today, magnesium metal is manufactured by the electrolysis of liquid magnesium chloride.

Which statements correctly describe what happens during this process?

Tick the correct boxes.

Liquid magnesium metal forms at the positive electrode. ☐

An electric current decomposes the electrolyte. ☐

An electric current passes through liquid magnesium chloride. ☐

Chlorine gas is made. ☐ [2]

H

ii During the electrolysis, magnesium ions form magnesium atoms.

Complete the symbol equation for the reaction.

Mg^{2+} _____ [2]

Total [12]

4 The lithosphere contains large amounts of silicon dioxide.

    a Finish the sentences about the structure of silicon dioxide.

       Choose words from this list.

simple	giant	weak	strong

       Silicon dioxide has a _____ covalent structure.

       Its atoms are held together by _____ covalent bonds.   [2]

    b This is a list of properties of silicon dioxide.

       A It has a high boiling point.

       B Solid and liquid silicon dioxide do not conduct electricity.

       C It is very hard.

       D It is insoluble in water.

       E It has a high melting point.

       Which properties best explain the following facts about silicon dioxide?

       Choose from the letters **A, B, C, D,** and **E**.

       i Silicon dioxide is used as an abrasive to make surfaces smooth.

         _____   [1]

       ii Silicon dioxide is used to line furnaces that heat things to very high temperatures.

         _____   [1]

    c Amethyst is a purple gemstone.

       It consists of silicon dioxide coloured by very small amounts of manganese and iron oxides.

       Give two properties that explain why amethyst is expensive.

       _____

       _____   [2]

                                                               Total [6]

1 Use these words to fill in the gaps.

electrons	negatively	attractive	repel	negative	positive

If you rub a balloon on your jumper, the balloon becomes charged. _____

have moved from your jumper to the balloon. Electrons are _____ charged.

So now the balloon has a _____ charge and your jumper has a

_____ charge.

If you hold the charged balloon close to your jumper, it tries to move towards your

jumper. This is because there are _____ forces between objects with

opposite charges.

If you hold two balloons with the same charge close to each other, they try to move

apart. This is because like charges _____.

2 Draw lines to join the beginnings of the sentences to the endings.

Draw one or more lines from each beginning.

Beginnings
All conductors . . .
Insulators . . .
Metal conductors . . .
In a complete circuit . . .

Endings
do not conduct electricity
include polythene, wood and rubber
charges are not used up
the battery makes free charges flow in a continuous loop
contain charges that are free to move
contain electrons that are free to move
do not contain charges that are free to move

3 Draw a (ring) round the correct bold words.

Resistors get **colder / hotter** when electric current flows through them. This is why lamp filaments glow.

The effect is caused by collisions between **moving / stationary** charges and **moving / stationary** atoms in the metal wire.

The resistance of a light dependent resistor (LDR) changes with light intensity. Its resistance in the dark is **less / more** than its resistance in the light.

The resistance of a thermistor changes with temperature. Usually, the higher the temperature, the **smaller / bigger** the resistance.

4 Fill in the empty boxes.

Component	Symbol
	Ⓐ
voltmeter	
battery (or cell)	
power supply	
	⊗
switch	
light dependent resistor (LDR)	
fixed resistor	
	▱ (with arrow)
thermistor	

5 In the six circuits below, all the lamps are identical.

For each pair of circuits, draw a ⟨ring⟩ round the circuit in which the ammeter reading is greater.

a

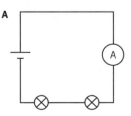

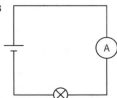

b

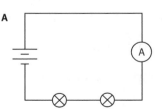

c

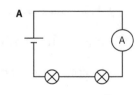

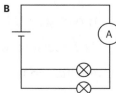

6 Write the letters of the statements below in a sensible place on the Venn diagram.

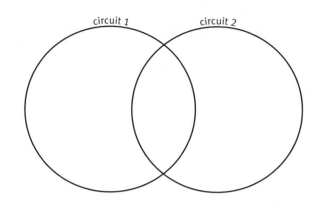

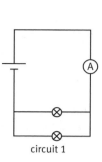

circuit 1

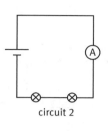

circuit 2

A The battery pushes all the charges through all the lamps.

B There are several paths for charges to flow along.

C This circuit has a greater total resistance.

D The ammeter reading is smaller for this circuit.

E The components resist the flow of charge through them.

F The total resistance is smaller for this circuit.

G The resistance of the connecting wires is so small that you can ignore it.

H It is easier for the battery to push charges round this circuit.

7 Calculate the resistances of the bulbs.

a

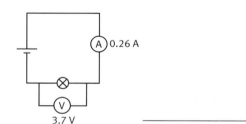

3.7 V _____

b

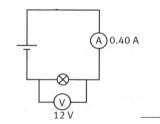

12 V _____

8 **a** In this circuit, the voltage is 230 V. The resistance of the fridge-freezer is 575 Ω.

What is the reading on the ammeter?

_____

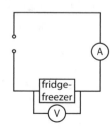

b This is the circuit in a simple torch.

What battery voltage would make a current of 0.5 A flow through the lamp?

_____

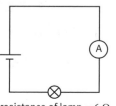

resistance of lamp = 6 Ω

9 Fill in the gaps.

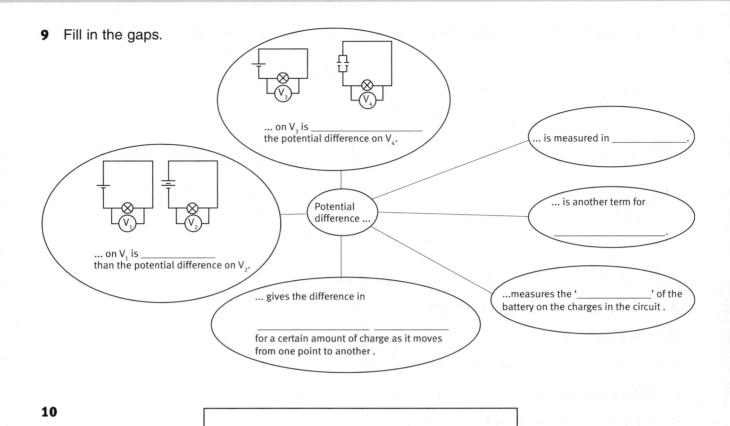

... on V_3 is _____ the potential difference on V_4.

... on V_1 is _____ than the potential difference on V_2.

Potential difference ...

... is measured in _____.

... is another term for

_____.

... gives the difference in

_____ _____ for a certain amount of charge as it moves from one point to another.

...measures the '_____' of the battery on the charges in the circuit.

10

V₄   A₁

100 mA

A₃   A₂

V₁   V₂   V₃
0.1 V   0.2 V   0.3 V

a On the diagram, write the readings on ammeters A₁ and A₂.

H **b** **i** On the diagram, draw a (ring) round the resistor that has the greatest resistance.

ii Draw a (ring) round the correct bold word below. Then complete the sentence.

The potential difference is **smallest / greatest** across the

component with the greatest resistance because

_____

c **i** On the diagram, write the reading on voltmeter V₄.

ii Complete the sentence:

I know that this is the voltage on V₄ because _____

_____

_____

11 Fill in the empty boxes. Use the right-hand column to work out your answers.

Appliance	Power rating (W)	Power rating (kW)	Time it is on for	Energy transferred (kWh)	Working
computer	250	0.250	2 hours		
kettle	1800	1.800	3 minutes		
toaster			5 minutes	0.10	
mobile phone charger			2 hours	0.04	

12 One unit (kWh) of electricity costs 10p.

Calculate the cost of using the following electrical items.

a A 1.9 kW washing machine for 1.25 hours:

Answer: _____

b A 0.5 kW surround sound system for 2 hours:

Answer: _____

13 Fill in the gaps.

If you move the magnet into the coil of wire, a voltage

is induced across the ends of the _____.

A _____ flows round the circuit.

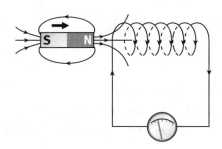

You can induce a voltage in the opposite direction by

moving the magnet _____ of the coil or

by moving the other _____ of the magnet

into the coil.

14 Calculate the current through these appliances.

The mains voltage in the UK is 230 V.

a A vacuum cleaner with a power rating of 900 W:

Answer: _____

b A DVD player with a power rating of 200 W:

Answer: _____

15 Calculate the voltage across the secondary coil.

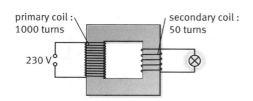

Answer: _____

16 Solve the clues to fill in the arrow words.

1 →							2 ↓	
3 →		4 →					5 →	
					← 6		16 ↓	
7 →								
8 →							← 9	
10 →							11 →	
12 →				13 →			14 →	
15 →								

Horizontal

1 Divide the voltage by the current to calculate this.

3 Home electricity meters measure energy transfer in

_____

4 The rate at which work is done by the battery on the components in a circuit.

5 The symbol for the unit of potential difference.

6 In this type of circuit, the current through each component is the same as if it were the only component.

7 Use this device to measure potential difference across a component in a circuit.

8 The symbol for the unit of resistance.

9 This device consists of a magnet rotating within a coil of wire.

10 Generators produce electricity by electromagnetic _____

11 The symbol for resistance.

12 Batteries produce _____ current.

13 This type of current reverses direction several times a second.

14 The symbol for the unit of electric current.

15 The percentage of energy supplied to a device that is usefully transferred.

Vertical

2 A flow of charge.

16 The abbreviation for direct current is _____.

Static electricity

If you rub a balloon in your hair, the balloon and your hair become charged. Tiny negative particles (electrons) move from your hair to the balloon.

Each hair is positively charged. Like charges repel. So the hairs get as far away from each other as possible.

There are attractive forces between opposite charges. So positively charged hairs are attracted to the negatively charged balloon.

Electric current

Electric current is a flow of charge.

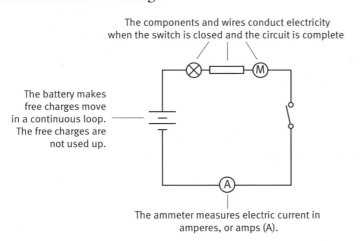

The components and wires conduct electricity when the switch is closed and the circuit is complete

The battery makes free charges move in a continuous loop. The free charges are not used up.

The ammeter measures electric current in amperes, or amps (A).

Metal conductors have many charges (electrons) that are free to move. Electric current is the movement of these free electrons.

Insulators do not conduct electricity. This is because they have no charges that are free to move.

Resistance

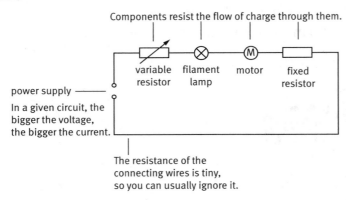

Components resist the flow of charge through them.

variable resistor · filament lamp · motor · fixed resistor

power supply ——

In a given circuit, the bigger the voltage, the bigger the current.

The resistance of the connecting wires is tiny, so you can usually ignore it.

For any circuit, the bigger the resistance, the smaller the current.

The current through a metal conductor is proportional to the voltage across it:

$$\textbf{resistance } (\text{ohm, } \Omega) = \frac{\textbf{voltage } (\text{volt, V})}{\textbf{current } (\text{ampere, A})}$$

current (A) | voltage (V)

The gradient of the graph is constant.

Resistors get hotter when electric current passes through them.

H This happens because moving electrons bump into stationary atoms in the wire.

Lamp filaments get so hot that they glow.

▶ Two resistors in series have more resistance than one on its own. The battery must now push charges through both resistors.

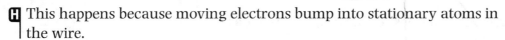

▶ Two resistors in parallel have a smaller total resistance than one on its own. There are now more paths for electric charges to flow along.

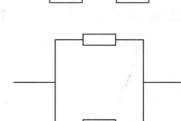

The resistance of a light dependent resistor (**LDR**) changes with light intensity. Its resistance in the dark is greater than its resistance in the light.

LDRs are useful for switching outdoor lights on at night and off in the morning.

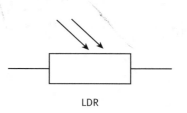

LDR

The resistance of a **thermistor** changes with temperature. For many thermistors, the hotter the temperature, the lower the resistance.

Thermistors are useful for switching water heaters on and off.

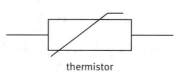

thermistor

Series and parallel circuits

The **voltage** of a battery shows its 'push' on the charges in a circuit.
Potential difference (p.d.) means the same as voltage.

Potential difference is the difference in potential energy, for each unit of charge flowing, between two points in a circuit.

Connect a **voltmeter** like this (see right) to measure the potential difference across a component:

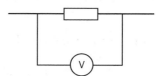

The readings on the voltmeter and ammeter are greater in circuit Y than in circuit X (see right). The second battery gives an extra 'push' to the charges in the circuit.

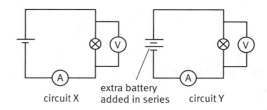

circuit X   extra battery added in series   circuit Y

H The readings on the voltmeter and ammeter are the same in circuits A and B (see right). The second battery in circuit B provides no extra 'push' to the charges in the circuit.

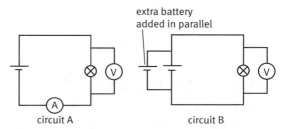

extra battery added in parallel

circuit A   circuit B

In circuit S, three components are connected in series to a battery. In circuit P, three components are connected in parallel to a battery.

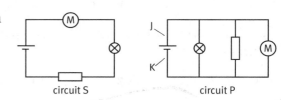

circuit S   circuit P

In circuit S . . .

▸ The same current flows through each component.

▸ The p.d.s across the components add up to the p.d. across the battery.

H This is because the work done by the battery on the electrons is the same as the work done on the electrons on the components.

▸ The p.d. is biggest across the component with the greatest resistance.

H This is because more work is done by charge flowing through a large resistance than through a small one.

In circuit P . . .

▸ The current at J, and at K, is equal to the sum of the currents through the components.

▸ The current is smallest through the component with the biggest resistance.

H The same battery voltage pushes more current through a component with a smaller resistance than through one with a bigger resistance.

▸ The current through each component is the same as if it were the only component in the circuit.

▸ The p.d. across each component is the same as the battery's p.d.

Electromagnetic induction

If you move a magnet into a coil of wire, a voltage
is induced across the ends of the coil. This is
electromagnetic induction. If you join up
the ends of the coil to make a circuit, a current
flows round the circuit.

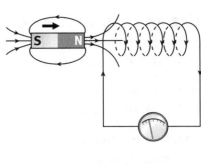

You can induce a voltage in the opposite direction by

▶ moving the magnet *out* of the coil, or

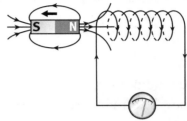

▶ moving the *other pole* of the magnet into the coil

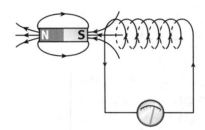

Generating mains electricity

Generators make electricity by electromagnetic induction.
In a generator, a magnet or electromagnet turns near a coil
of wire. This induces a voltage across the ends of the coil.

The direction of this voltage changes each time the magnet
rotates.

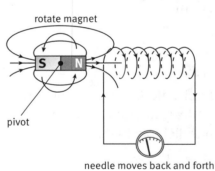

rotate magnet

pivot

needle moves back and forth

You can increase the size of the induced voltage by

▶ turning the magnet faster
▶ increasing the strength of the magnetic field
▶ adding more turns to the coil
▶ putting an iron core inside the coil

Alternating current

H The magnet in a generator turns all the time. Its magnetic field
constantly changes direction. So the direction of the induced current
changes all the time. This is an **alternating current (a.c.)**.

The current from a battery does not change direction. It is a **direct
current (d.c.)**.

Mains electricity is supplied as an alternating current (a.c.).

H This is because

▶ it is easier to generate than d.c.
▶ it can be distributed more efficiently, with less energy
wasted as heat

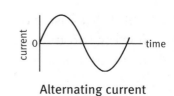

current

0

time

Alternating current

Transformers

A transformer changes the size of an alternating voltage. It consists of two coils of wire wound onto an iron core.

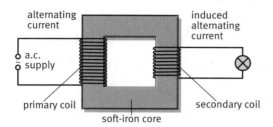

The voltage in the primary coil changes all the time. So it becomes a strong magnet. It induces a voltage in the secondary coil, where a current now flows.

H You can use this equation to work out the size of the voltage across the secondary coil:

$$\frac{\text{voltage across primary coil } (V_P)}{\text{voltage across secondary coil } (V_S)} = \frac{\text{number of turns on primary coil } (N_P)}{\text{number of turns on secondary coil } (N_S)}$$

The **National Grid** distributes electricity all over Britain. It uses transformers to change the voltage. Transmitting at very high voltage (so that the current is small) minimizes the amount of energy lost as heat.

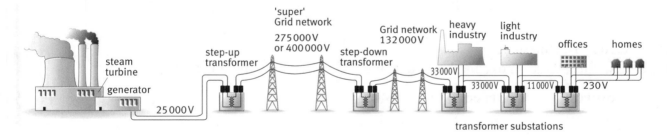

Electricity at home

Power

When electric current flows through a device, such as a computer, energy is transferred by the device.

The **power** of an appliance is the rate at which energy is transferred to it. Different appliances have different power ratings.

Energy transfer

You can use this equation to calculate the energy transferred to a device:

$$\textbf{energy transferred} \quad = \quad \textbf{power} \quad \times \quad \textbf{time}$$

energy transferred	power	time
(joule, J)	(watt, W)	(second, s)
(kilowatt hour, kWh)	(kilowatt, kW)	(hour, h)

For example, Rashid uses a computer with a power rating of 250 W for 10 minutes.

$$\text{energy transferred} \quad = \quad 250\ \text{W} \quad \times \quad (10 \times 60)\ \text{s}$$
$$= \quad 150\,000\ \text{J}$$

Jason spends half an hour ironing shirts. His iron has a power rating of 3 kW.

$$\text{energy transferred} \quad = \quad 3\ \text{kW} \quad \times \quad 0.5\ \text{h}$$
$$= \quad 1.5\ \text{kWh}$$

Paying for electricity

Home electricity meters measure energy transfer in kilowatt hours (kWh). One kWh is one unit of electricity.

$$\textbf{cost} \quad = \quad \textbf{number of units} \quad \times \quad \textbf{cost of one unit}$$

If one unit costs 10p, then the cost of Jason's ironing is

$$\text{cost} \quad = \quad 1.5\ \text{kWh} \quad \times \quad 10\text{p} \quad = \quad 15.0\text{p}$$

Current through appliances

You can use this equation to calculate the current through an appliance:

$$\textbf{power} \quad = \quad \textbf{current} \quad \times \quad \textbf{voltage}$$

power	current	voltage
(watt, W)	(ampere, A)	(volt, V)

H For example, the power rating of a hairdryer is 1000 W. The mains voltage in the UK is 230 V. Rearranging the equation gives

$$\text{current} \quad = \quad \frac{\text{power}}{\text{voltage}} \quad = \quad \frac{1000\ \text{W}}{230\ \text{V}} \quad = \quad 4.3\ \text{A}$$

Efficiency

You can use this equation to calculate the efficiency of an appliance:

$$\textbf{efficiency} \quad = \quad \frac{\textbf{energy usefully transferred}}{\textbf{total energy supplied}} \quad \times \quad \textbf{100\%}$$

For example, a 100 W filament lamp transfers 10 J of energy as light each second.

The total energy supplied by electricity is 100 J.

So the efficiency of the filament lamp is $\dfrac{10\ \text{J}}{100\ \text{J}} \times 100\% = 10\%$

1   Vanessa makes a model fire engine for her little sister, Ursula.
She connects the circuit shown in the diagram.

When the switch is closed the lamp lights and the siren sounds.

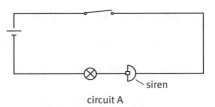

circuit A

a   Which of the following statements are correct?

Tick each of the correct boxes.

When the switch is closed, the battery makes free charges
in the circuit move.   ☐

The metal wires contain electrons that are free to move.   ☐

When the switch is closed, atoms in the light filament are
free to move.   ☐

Electrons are positively charged.   ☐

When the switch is closed there is a flow of charge. This is
an electric current.   ☐

When a current flows in the circuit, free charges are used up.   ☐   [2]

b   Ursula wants the light to be brighter.

Vanessa connects these circuits.

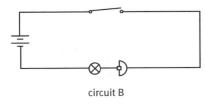

circuit B

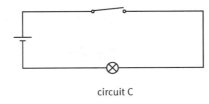

circuit C

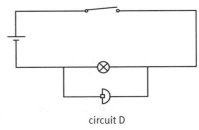

circuit D

In each circuit, the light is brighter than it was in circuit A.

Explain why, by choosing words from this list to complete the sentences.

voltage	**current**	**resistance**

The lamp in circuit B is brighter because the _____ of the

battery is bigger. So the _____ in the circuit is bigger.

The lamp in circuit C is brighter because the siren has been removed.

The total _____ of the circuit is less so the _____

is bigger.

The lamp in circuit D is brighter because there are more paths for the

charges to flow along. The _____ is bigger because the total

_____ is less.   [3]

Total [5]

2 Tamara has a portable heater. She plugs it into a car battery.

She puts the heating element into a mug of water to make a hot drink.

a Tamara wants to find out more about her heater.

She connects this circuit.

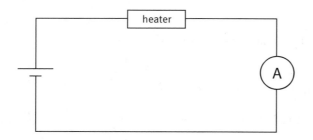

i Tamara uses a voltmeter to measure the voltage across the heater.

Draw on the diagram to show where to connect the voltmeter.

Use the correct symbol. [1]

ii The reading on the voltmeter is 12 V. The ammeter reads 10 A.

Calculate the resistance of the heater.

Resistance = _____ Ohms [2]

b The heater contains a heating element made from a coil of wire.

The wire gets hotter when an electric current passes through it.

Explain why the wire gets hotter.

_____

_____

_____ [2]

Total [5]

3 **a** Amir has a fridge-freezer. He leaves it on all the time.

Its power rating is 90 W, which is equal to 0.09 kW.

Calculate the energy transferred by the fridge-freezer in one year.

There are 8760 hours in a year.

Energy transferred = _____ kWh   [2]

b The French Environment Agency calculated that washing, tumble drying and ironing a pair of jeans every three weeks for a year transfers 240 kWh of energy as electricity.

The cost of one unit of electricity in France is 0.10.

Calculate the cost of washing jeans for a year in France.

Answer = _____   [2]

c Over a year, an average British household spends £27 on running its washing machine.

One unit of electricity costs £0.10.

The power rating of an average washing machine is 1.10 kW.

Calculate how many units are used.

Calculate the total length of time for which an average British household uses its washing machine over a year.

Answer = _____ hours   [4]

Total [8]

4 The diagram shows part of an electric circuit in Matt's house.

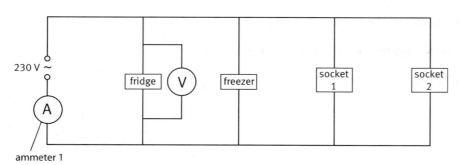

a i What is the reading on the voltmeter connected across the fridge?

_____

[1]

ii What is the potential difference across the fridge?

_____

[1]

b The resistance of the freezer is 70 Ω.

The voltage across the freezer is 230 V.

Calculate the current through the freezer.

Current = _____ amps [2]

c Matt plugs a kettle into socket 1.

What happens to the size the current through the freezer?

Draw a (ring) around the correct answer.

increases   decreases   stays the same

[1]

H

d Matt plugs a kettle into socket 1 and an electric heater into socket 2.

He switches off the freezer.

He measures the currents through the appliances that are switched on.

Appliance	Current (A)
fridge	0.4
kettle	5.0
heater	9.0

i What current flows through ammeter 1?

Current = _____ amps   [2]

ii Which appliance in the table has the greatest resistance?

_____   [1]

Give a reason for your answer.

_____

_____   [1]

Total [9]

5 Scientists are developing a wind-up laptop computer. School students will use it in places where electricity supplies are not reliable.

A person turns a handle for 1 minute. This winds up a spring.

Then the spring unwinds slowly. This rotates a magnet within a coil of wire.

An electric current is produced.

a Suggest three changes the scientists could make to the generator so that it produced a bigger current.

Change 1: _____

Change 2: _____

Change 3: _____   [3]

b The computer can also be plugged into the mains electricity supply.

A transformer changes the size of the voltage.

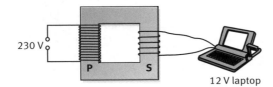

i Complete the sentences to explain how the transformer works.

Two coils of wire are wound onto an _____ core.

There is a changing magnetic field around coil P.

This _____ a voltage in coil S.   [2]

ii Coil P has 2300 turns.

Calculate the number of turns needed in coil S so that the voltage across the computer is 12 V.

Answer = _____   [2]

Total [7]

1 Match each word with its definition.

Word
behaviour
stimulus
response

Definition
A change in the environment
An action caused by a change in the environment
Anything an animal does

2 Each picture shows one newborn reflex.

Add a caption to each picture that **names and describes** the reflex.

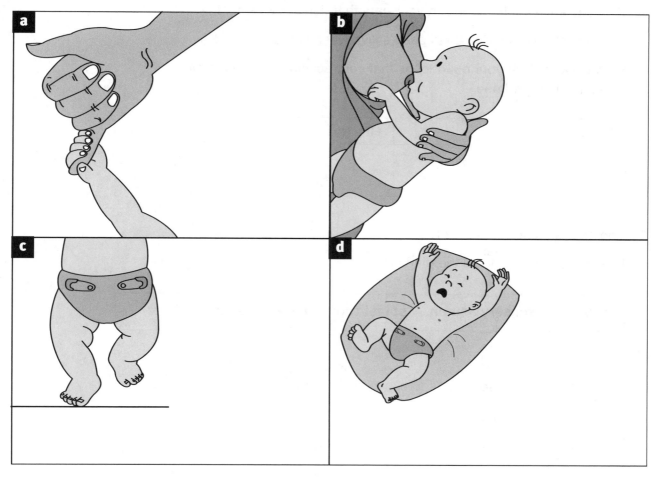

3 Write **S** next to the sentences that best apply to simple animals, like woodlice.

Write **C** next to the sentences that best apply to complex animals, like horses.

a These animals rely on reflex actions for most of their behaviour.

b These animals can change their behaviour.

c These animals find it difficult to respond to new situations.

d These animals are less likely to survive environmental changes.

These animals can learn to link a new stimulus to a reflex action.

4 Write the letters of the receptors and effectors below in the correct column of the table.

A Skin cells that detect pain

B Cells in your retina that detect light

C Muscle cells in a baby's fingers that make him grip your finger tightly

D A sweat gland that releases sweat when you are nervous

E Taste buds on your tongue

F The semi-circular canals in your ears that detect movement

G The salivary gland that releases saliva when you smell food

H Muscle cells in your quadriceps that contract when someone hits you below the knee

Receptors	Effectors

5 The diagram shows a reflex arc.

Use these words to label the diagram.

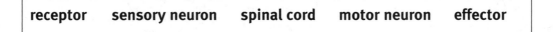

| receptor | sensory neuron | spinal cord | motor neuron | effector |

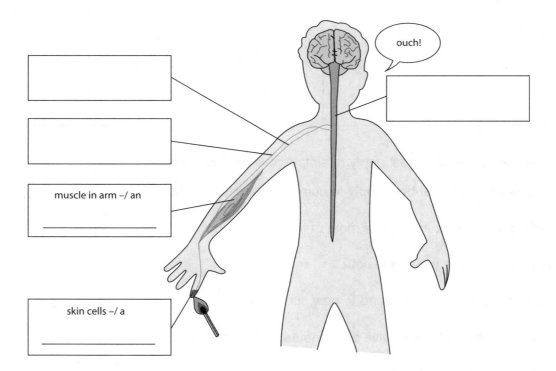

muscle in arm –/ an

skin cells –/ a

6 The stages below describe how information is passed along a simple reflex arc. They are in the wrong order.

A A receptor cell detects dust in your eye.

B The effectors (muscles in your eyelid) blink to remove the dust.

C The CNS receives the impulses.

D The CNS processes the information.

E The CNS sends an electrical impulse along a motor neuron to the effectors.

F A sensory neuron carries electrical impulses to your central nervous system (CNS).

Fill in the boxes to show the correct order. The first one has been done for you.

| A | | | | | |

7 The diagram shows a motor neuron.

Complete the labels to describe what each part of the cell does.

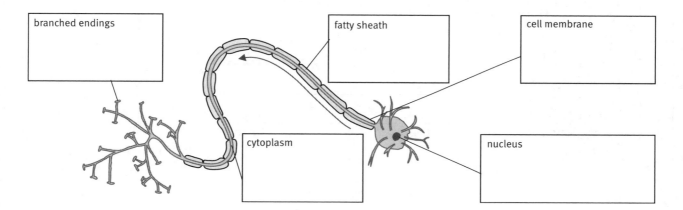

branched endings

fatty sheath

cell membrane

cytoplasm

nucleus

H **8** The cartoon shows the benefits of one conditioned reflex action.

Complete the thought bubbles to describe the benefits.

1 *Mmm... that red and yellow caterpillar looks delicious!*

2 *Good. She's learnt that lesson. It'll help her to survive because...*

Yuk! That's foul! It tastes revolting!

Excellent. That'll help me survive because...

H 9 The diagrams show how a nerve impulse crosses a synapse.
They are in the wrong order.

  ▸ Number each box to show the correct sequence.

  ▸ Write notes next to each diagram to explain the process.

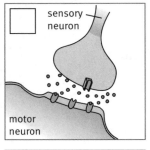

_____

_____

_____

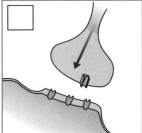

_____

_____

_____

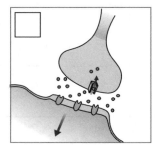

_____

_____

_____

10 The statements below are about memory.

Write the letter for each statement in
the correct part of the Venn diagram.

  A This lasts about 30 seconds.

  B This can last a lifetime.

  C There is a limit to how much we can
  remember here.

  D There is no limit to how much we can
  remember here.

  E This is the storage and retrieval of information
  by the brain.

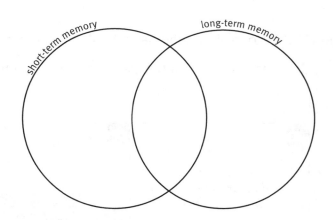

11 The diagram shows the human brain.

Complete the sentences.

a Your cerebral cortex is concerned with

C _____

L _____

I _____

M _____

b Different areas of the cortex have different jobs.

Scientists have mapped these areas by _____

_____.

c You have many potential pathways in your brain so you can

_____

_____.

d Your brain has billions of n _____.

They are connected together in complicated p _____.

12 The stages below describe how new pathways develop in your brain when you learn to ice skate.

They are in the wrong order.

A You ice skate for the first time.

B More impulses go along the same pathway.

C There is now a new connection between the neurons.

D Nerve impulses travel along the pathway more easily.

E You go ice skating again.

F A nerve travels along a certain pathway, from one neuron to another, for the first time.

G The connection between the neurons gets stronger.

H You now find it much easier to ice skate.

Fill in the boxes to show the correct order.

The first one has been done for you.

| A | | | | | | | |

13 Solve the clues to fill in the arrow word.

Horizontal

3 Being aware of yourself and your surroundings.

5 An explanation for how human memory works.

6 Going over something again and again helps you to learn by _____.

7 A place where you can buy things!

8 The biceps _____ in your right arm is an effector.

9 _____ children do not learn to speak.

10 A long, thin extension of the cytoplasm of a neuron.

11 The brain and spinal cord form the _____.

12 This part of the brain is concerned with consciousness, memory, language, and intelligence.

13 The symbol for nitrogen.

14 In the brain, neurons are connected in _____.

15 This sort of memory lasts about 30 seconds.

16 No _____ of memory gives a full explanation of how memory works.

17 A _____ studies how the brain works.

Vertical

1 Some brain synapses release this chemical. It gives a feeling of pleasure.

2 A tiny gap between neurons.

3 The _____ cortex is concerned with memory, intelligence, consciousness, and learning.

4 A nerve cell.

15 A change in the environment that causes a response.

Responding to changes in the environment

You are at a party. As more people arrive, the room gets hotter. You start to sweat more.

A change in your environment, or **stimulus** (the increase in temperature), has triggered a **response** (increased sweating). Sweating is an example of **behaviour**. Behaviour is an animal's response to stimuli; it is everything an animal does.

Animals respond to stimuli to keep themselves in conditions that help them survive.

Simple reflex actions

If you walk into a dark room, your pupils immediately get bigger. This is a **simple reflex action**. Reflexes are automatic, or **involuntary**. They happen very quickly.

Simple reflexes make animals respond to stimuli in ways that help them survive. They help animals to

- find food
- find a mate
- escape or shelter from predators

Simple animals rely on reflex actions for most of their behaviour. So they always respond in the same way to a particular stimulus. For example, woodlice move away from light.

It is difficult for simple animals to respond to new situations. So they often fail to survive environmental changes.

A human baby shows **newborn reflexes**, including

- **grasping** – tightly gripping a finger in their palm
- **sucking** a nipple or finger in their mouth
- **stepping** when their feet touch a flat surface
- **startling** – spreading out arms and legs when they hear a loud noise

Babies gradually replace these reflexes with behaviours learned from experience.

The **pupil reflex** stops bright light damaging sensitive cells in the retina.

Simple animals always respond to a stimulus in the same way. These woodlice are moving away from the light.

- In bright light, muscles in the iris contract. The pupil gets smaller, so less light enters the eye.

- In dim light, different muscles in the iris contract. The pupil gets bigger, so more light enters the eye.

⊞ Conditioned reflex actions

Complex animals can learn to link a new stimulus to a reflex action. So they can change their behaviour.

For example, Pavlov taught a dog to salivate when it heard a bell ring:

▶ The dog's simple reflex was to salivate when it was given food.
▶ Pavlov rang a bell while the dog was eating.
▶ After a while, the dog salivated every time it heard the bell – even if there was no food!

The stimulus (hearing the bell) became linked to food. The stimulus led to the reflex action of salivating. The final response had no direct connection to the stimulus. This is a **conditioned reflex action**.

Conditioned reflexes increase an animal's chance of survival. For example, many bitter-tasting caterpillars are brightly coloured. When a bird tastes these caterpillars, it learns not to eat them. If the caterpillar is poisonous, this conditioned reflex makes the bird more likely to survive, too.

The nervous system

The reflex arc

In a simple reflex, nerve cells carry **nerve impulses** from one part of the **nervous system** to the next. This pathway is the **reflex arc**.

▶ A **receptor** cell detects a stimulus.
▶ A **sensory neuron** carries nerve impulses as electrical signals to the **central nervous system** (**CNS**).
▶ The CNS is the brain and spinal cord. It coordinates responses to stimuli.
▶ A **motor neuron** carries nerve impulses as electrical signals from the CNS to an **effector**.
▶ The effector takes action in response to the stimulus.

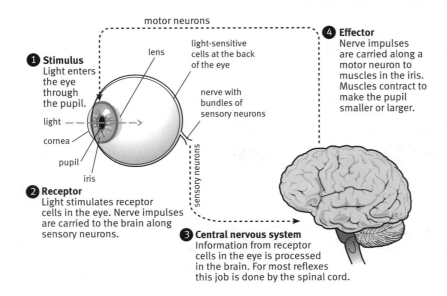

motor neurons

1 Stimulus
Light enters the eye through the pupil.

lens

light-sensitive cells at the back of the eye

4 Effector
Nerve impulses are carried along a motor neuron to muscles in the iris. Muscles contract to make the pupil smaller or larger.

nerve with bundles of sensory neurons

light

cornea

pupil

iris

sensory neurons

2 Receptor
Light stimulates receptor cells in the eye. Nerve impulses are carried to the brain along sensory neurons.

3 Central nervous system
Information from receptor cells in the eye is processed in the brain. For most reflexes this job is done by the spinal cord.

An example of a reflex arc

The peripheral nervous system

The sensory and motor neurons of the **peripheral nervous system** link the CNS to the rest of the body.

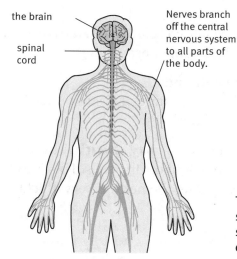

the brain

spinal cord

Nerves branch off the central nervous system to all parts of the body.

The peripheral nervous system links the brain and spinal cord with the rest of the body.

Receptors

Receptors include:

▶ single cells, such as pain sensor cells in the skin

▶ cells in complex organs, such as **light-sensitive cells** in the retina. These detect light and send nerve impulses along neurons to the brain.

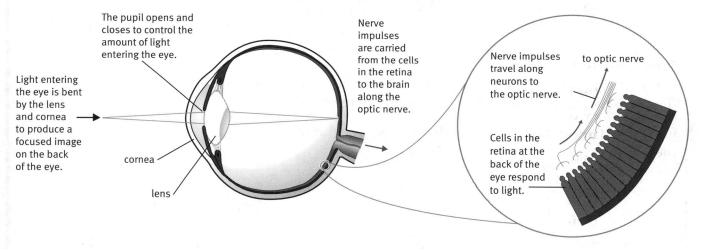

The pupil opens and closes to control the amount of light entering the eye.

Light entering the eye is bent by the lens and cornea to produce a focused image on the back of the eye.

cornea

lens

Nerve impulses are carried from the cells in the retina to the brain along the optic nerve.

Nerve impulses travel along neurons to the optic nerve.

to optic nerve

Cells in the retina at the back of the eye respond to light.

Light is focused by the cornea and lens onto light-sensitive cells at the back of the eye. These cells are receptors. They trigger nerve impulses to the brain.

Effectors

Effectors are either **muscles** or **glands**. When they are stimulated by nerve impulses:

▶ muscle cells contract to move a part of the body – for example, you 'gag' when something touches the back of your throat

▶ glands release chemicals, for example sweat or hormones

Neurons

Nerves are bundles of specialized cells called **neurons**. Neurons have a nucleus, cytoplasm, and a cell membrane.

▶ The nucleus is in the **cell body**.

▶ The cytoplasm is a long, thin fibre. It is surrounded by the cell membrane. This is the **axon**.

Some axons are surrounded by a **fatty sheath**. The fatty sheath insulates the neuron from neighbouring cells. This means that electrical nerve impulses can travel along the neuron very quickly.

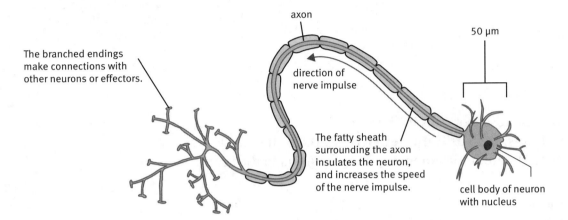

A motor neuron

The branched endings make connections with other neurons or effectors.

axon

direction of nerve impulse

50 μm

The fatty sheath surrounding the axon insulates the neuron, and increases the speed of the nerve impulse.

cell body of neuron with nucleus

Synapses

Synapses are tiny gaps between neurons. Nerve impulses must cross these gaps when they travel from one neuron to the next.

H Chemicals pass an impulse across the synapse from one neuron to the next.

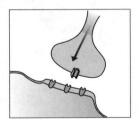

1 A nerve impulse gets to the end of a sensory neuron.

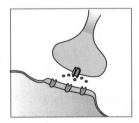

2 The sensory neuron releases a chemical into the synapse.

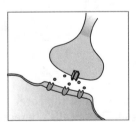

3 The chemical diffuses across the synapse.

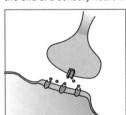

4 The chemical arrives at receptor molecules on the motor neuron's membrane. The chemical's molecules are the correct shape to bind to the receptor molecules.

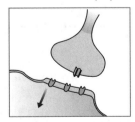

5 A nerve impulse is stimulated in the motor neuron.

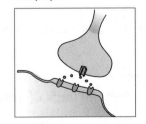

6 The chemical is absorbed back into the sensory neuron to be used again.

Some drugs and poisons affect the transmission of nerve impulses across synapses.

H The chemical **serotonin** is released at some synapses in the brain. This gives a feeling of pleasure. Sensory neurons later remove the serotonin. This is a natural process.

The drug **Ecstasy** (MDMA) blocks the places that remove serotonin. So the serotonin concentration in the synapse increases. This can make Ecstasy users feel happy for a while. But Ecstasy is very harmful. It interferes with temperature control systems and can kill. Long-term users suffer anxiety and depression.

Consciously controlling reflexes

Sometimes the brain consciously changes a reflex response. For example:

▶ You pick up a hot plate of delicious food. A nerve impulse travels along a sensory neuron to your spinal cord. Your reflex response is to drop the plate.

▶ But another nerve impulse travels up your spine to your brain. It comes back down to the motor neuron and makes a muscle movement in your arm that stops the reflex response.

▶ You keep hold of the plate until you can put it down safely.

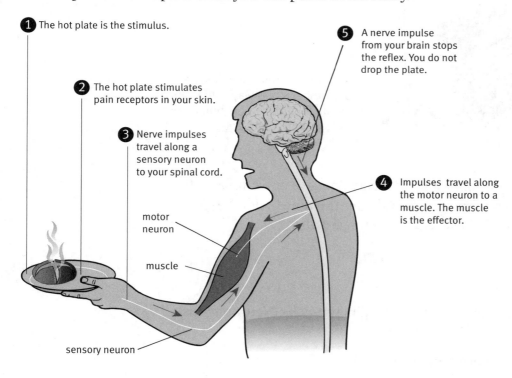

1 The hot plate is the stimulus.

2 The hot plate stimulates pain receptors in your skin.

3 Nerve impulses travel along a sensory neuron to your spinal cord.

5 A nerve impulse from your brain stops the reflex. You do not drop the plate.

4 Impulses travel along the motor neuron to a muscle. The muscle is the effector.

motor neuron

muscle

sensory neuron

Developing complex behaviour

Mammals – including humans – can change their behaviour as a result of new experiences. This is **learning**.

Mammals have complex brains with billions of neurons. The neurons are connected together in complicated **pathways**. Learning new things creates new pathways. There are many potential pathways in the brain. So animals can adapt to new situations and learn to interact effectively with others.

New pathways develop as a result of practice and repetition.

▸ You experience something new.

▸ A nerve impulse travels along a particular pathway, from one neuron to another, for the first time. There are new connections between the neurons.

▸ You repeat the experience.

▸ More impulses go along the same pathway. The connections between the neurons get stronger.

▸ Nerve impulses travel along the pathway more easily. It is easier to respond in the way that you practised.

As the drummer practises, he strengthens pathways between certain neurons in his brain. So he gets better and better!

Children can only acquire some skills at a certain age. For example, a **feral** (wild) child cannot learn to speak if found after the time in development when they would normally have learnt language skills.

The cortex
Mapping the cortex
Different regions of the brain's cortex have different jobs. Neuroscientists map the cortex by:

▸ studying patients with brain damage

▸ electrically stimulating different parts of the brain

▸ doing MRI scans of the brain – these show which parts of the brain are most active when a person does different things

The **cerebral cortex** is the region most concerned with intelligence, language, memory, and **consciousness** (being aware of yourself and your surroundings).

Memory

Memory is the storage and retrieval of information by the brain. Verbal **memory** is stored information about words and language.

There are two types of verbal memory. They work separately in the brain.

▸ **Short-term memory** lasts about 30 seconds.

▸ **Long-term memory** is a seemingly limitless store of information that can last a lifetime.

Psychologists have devised various models to explain how memory works. One of these is called the **multistore** model. However, no model gives a full explanation.

Humans use different ways to help them remember information:

H ▸ Looking for patterns, or organizing information to make a pattern. If you can see a pattern, you process the information more deeply.

For example, Dan's shopping list is organized into groups. Jordan's list isn't. Most people would find it easier to remember Dan's shopping list.

apples
bananas
oranges

deodorant
razors
soap
shampoo

T-shirt
socks

Dan's list

deodorant
T-shirt
bananas
razors
soap
oranges
socks
apples
shampoo

Jordan's list

▸ Repeating the information as much as possible. For example, actors learn their lines by going over them again and again and again.

▸ Associating the information with a strong stimulus, for example light, colour, a smell, or music. So a whiff of perfume might remind you of a friend who wears that perfume, or a piece of music might bring back happy or sad memories.

1 This question is about reflex actions.

   a Sarah is five months old. Look at the list of things that she does.

     Tick the **two** actions that are newborn reflexes.

     She grips a finger that is put into the palm of her hand. ☐

     She stops crying when her sister sings to her. ☐

     She spreads out her arms and legs when she hears a sudden noise. ☐

     She cries when her favourite toy is taken away. ☐

     She goes to sleep in her pram. ☐ **[2]**

   b Until she was two months old, Sarah sucked anything that was put into her mouth.

     Complete the sentences.

     Sucking is the response to the stimulus of _____

     _____

     The newborn sucking reflex helped Sarah's survival by making sure

     she got enough _____. **[2]**

   c Humans rely on reflex actions for only some of their behaviour.

     Worms rely on reflex actions for most of their behaviour.

     Give one disadvantage of relying on simple reflex actions for most behaviour.

     _____

     _____ **[1]**

Total [5]

2 a Draw a line to match each part of the nervous system to its job.

Part of nervous system
effector cells
receptor cells
brain and spinal cord

Job
control the body's response to a stimulus
detect a stimulus
make changes in response to a stimulus

[2]

b Josh is crossing the road. He sees a car coming towards him.

A nerve signal travels from his eyes to his adrenal glands.

His adrenal glands release a hormone, adrenaline.

The adrenaline helps Josh to get out of the way of the car before it hits him.

i The path taken by the nerve signal is shown in the diagram.

Use these words to finish labelling the diagram.

sensory neuron	**motor neuron**	**central nervous system**

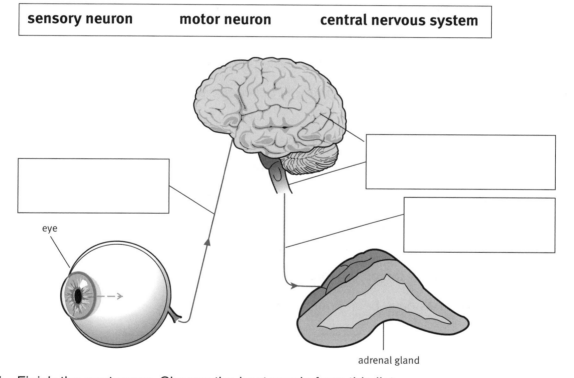

eye

adrenal gland

[3]

ii Finish the sentences. Choose the best words from this list.

Use each word once, more than once or not at all.

peripheral	**central**	**electrical**	**chemical**

The signal is carried along nerve cells by _____ impulses.

The sensory and motor neurons are part of the _____ nervous

system. The brain and spinal cord form the _____ nervous system.

[3]

Total [8]

3 Dolphins are mammals.

   a Dolphins can adapt to new situations.

     Tick the statement that **best** explains why.

       Dolphins have billions of neurons. ☐

       A dolphin's brain has a great variety of potential neuron
pathways. ☐

       Dolphins respond to stimuli by both simple and conditioned
reflex actions. ☐

       Dolphins can learn reflex responses to new stimuli. ☐

       The average dolphin's brain has a mass of 1.6 kg. ☐   **[1]**

   b The steps below describe how a dolphin learns to jump through
a hoop.

     They are in the wrong order.

     A The dolphin jumps through a hoop for the first time.

     B More nerve impulses travel along the same pathway.

     C A nerve impulse travels along a pathway between two
neurons in the brain for the first time.

     D The dolphin jumps through the hoop again.

     E This makes a connection between the two neurons.

     F This makes the connection between the two neurons stronger.

     G It is now easier for nerve impulses to travel along the pathway,
and so easier for the dolphin to jump through hoops.

     Fill in the boxes to show the correct order.

     The first and last ones have been done for you.

     | A | ☐ | ☐ | ☐ | ☐ | ☐ | G | **[4]**

                                                        Total [5]

H 4 a Louise has a cat called Tibbles.

When Tibbles hears Louise use a tin-opener, he produces saliva.

Finish the sentences. Choose the best words from this list.

Use each word once, more than once or not at all.

response	learned	conditioned	simple	stimulus

The sound of Louise using a tin-opener is the _____.

Tibbles production of saliva is the _____. The response

has no direct connection to the stimulus. Tibbles has _____

the response. So this is a _____ reflex action. [4]

b Wasps are insects. They are black and yellow.

  i A bird has learned that wasps taste bitter.

  The bird never eats black and yellow insects.

  Explain how this behaviour might help the bird survive.

  _____

  _____

  _____ [1]

  ii Hover flies are also black and yellow.

  They do not have a bitter taste.

  Explain how the hover fly's colouring helps it to survive.

  _____

  _____ [1]

  Total [6]

5 Synapses are gaps between neighbouring neurons.

a The statements describe how nerve impulses cross a synapse.

They are in the wrong order.

A A nerve impulse arrives at the synapse.

B Molecules of the chemical fit into receptor molecules on the motor neuron.

C A chemical is released from the sensory neuron.

D The chemical is absorbed back into the sensory neuron to be used again.

E The chemical diffuses across the synapse.

F A nerve impulse is stimulated in the motor neuron.

Fill in the boxes to show the correct order.

The first one has been done for you.

| A | ☐ | ☐ | ☐ | ☐ | ☐ |

[4]

b The drug Ecstasy affects the transmission of impulses across synapses.

Ticks the **two** statements that best explain how.

Ecstasy causes a decrease in the concentration of serotonin in the brain. ☐

Ecstasy makes it easier for synapses in the brain to remove serotonin. ☐

Ecstasy makes sensory neurons release more serotonin. ☐

Ecstasy causes an increase in the concentration of serotonin in the brain. ☐

Ecstasy blocks sites in the brain's synapses where serotonin is removed. ☐

Ecstasy makes sensory neurons release less serotonin. ☐

[2]

Total [6]

1 Write each from the box example in an appropriate place on the diagram.

paracetamol
polythene
saccharin (a sweetener)
ammonium nitrate

food additives e.g. _____

fertilizers e.g. _____

Chemical synthesis provides chemicals for...

pharmaceuticals e.g. _____

plastics e.g. _____

pigments e.g. titanium oxide

2 The pie chart shows the percentage value of products made by the British chemical industry.

Complete the sentences.

a Chemicals used in

_____ earn

the most money for the

British chemical industry.

b The total percentage

value of paints, varnishes,

printing inks, dyes and

pigments is _____.

c The percentage value of British fibres is _____% less than that

of soaps, toiletries, and cleaning preparations.

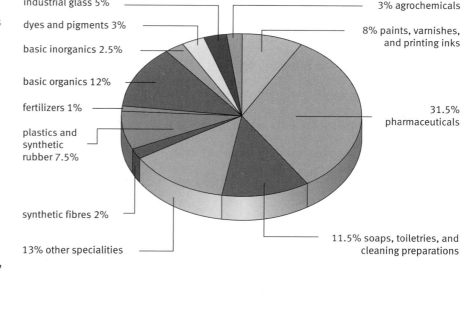

industrial glass 5%

dyes and pigments 3%

basic inorganics 2.5%

basic organics 12%

fertilizers 1%

plastics and synthetic rubber 7.5%

synthetic fibres 2%

13% other specialities

3% agrochemicals

8% paints, varnishes, and printing inks

31.5% pharmaceuticals

11.5% soaps, toiletries, and cleaning preparations

3 Fill in the empty boxes.

Name of chemical	Formula
nitrogen gas	
nitric acid	
	$MgSO_4$
	KCl

Name of chemical	Formula
calcium chloride	
	Na_2CO_3
calcium carbonate	

4 Write the names of these pure acids in the table.

tartaric
ethanoic
nitric
sulfuric
citric

gases	liquids	solids

5 For the sentences below

▶ write **acid** next to each sentence that is true for acids

▶ write **alkali** next to each sentence that is true for alkalis

▶ write **both** next to each sentence that is true for both acids and alkalis

a They have a pH less than 7. _____

b They produce OH^- ions when they dissolve in water. _____

c They make litmus indicator turn red. _____

d They neutralize acids. _____

e Wear eye protection when working with these. _____

f Drain cleaners contain one of these. _____

g Concentrated solutions of these are more dangerous than dilute solutions. _____

h They produce H^+ ions when they dissolve in water. _____

i Use a pH meter to measure the pH of solutions of these. _____

H **6** **a** Rock climbers put magnesium carbonate powder on their hands to increase friction between their hands and the rock.

The formula of magnesium carbonate is $MgCO_3$.

Carbonate ions have a charge of –2.

What is the charge on a magnesium ion? _____

b The formula of aluminium oxide is Al_2O_3.

The formula of an oxide ion is O^{2-}.

What is the charge on an aluminium ion? _____

7 Fill in the empty boxes.

Name of salt	Formula of acid used to make the salt	Formula of alkali used to make the salt	Formula of salt
potassium chloride	HCl	KOH	
sodium sulfate	H_2SO_4	NaOH	
calcium nitrate	HNO_3	$Ca(OH)_2$	
lithium chloride	HCl	LiOH	

8 The diagram shows apparatus for a titration.

Use the phrases in the box to label the diagram.

accurately weighed solid sample   **pure water**
titration flask   **acid or alkali**   **burette**

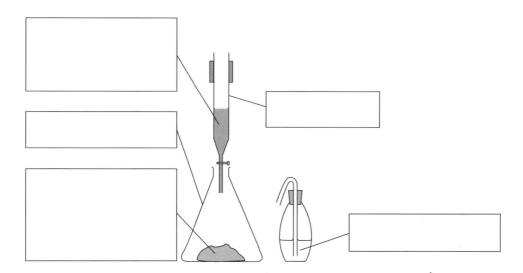

H **9** Balance the equations.

a NaOH + HCl → NaCl + H_2O

b KOH + H_2SO_4 → K_2SO_4 + H_2O

c Mg + O_2 → MgO

d Li + O_2 → Li_2O

e $AgNO_3$ + NaCl → AgCl + $NaNO_3$

f $Pb(NO_3)_2$ + KCl → $PbCl_2$ + KNO_3

g Fe_2O_3 + C → CO + Fe

h $CaCO_3$ → CaO + CO_2

10 Fill in the gaps in these equations.

  a acid + _____ → salt + hydrogen

  b acid + alkali → _____ + _____

  c acid + metal oxide → _____ + water

  d acid + carbonate → salt + _____ + _____

Finish adding state symbols to these equations. (All the reactions happen at room temperature.)

  e $2HNO_3(aq) + Na_2CO_3(s) → 2NaNO_3$ __ $+ CO_2$ __ $+ H_2O$ __

  f $H_2SO_4(aq) + 2KOH(aq) → K_2SO_4$ __ $+ 2H_2O$ __

  g $H_2SO_4(aq) + CaO(s) → CaSO_4$ __ $+ H_2O$ __

  h $2HCl(aq) + Mg(s) → MgCl_2$ __ $+ H_2$ __

In the table, match each reaction type from the equations above with one example.

Reaction type	Example (equations e to h)
a	
b	
c	
d	

11 Katie added lumps of calcium carbonate to hydrochloric acid.

The calcium carbonate and hydrochloric acid reacted together.

Katie did the reaction 6 more times.

Tick one column in each row to show how the reaction rate changed each time.

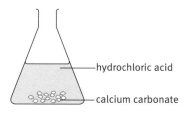
hydrochloric acid
calcium carbonate

Change	The reaction gets . . .		
	faster	slower	can't tell
a Use bigger lumps of calcium carbonate			
b Use more concentrated acid			
c Heat the reaction mixture			
d Use bigger lumps of calcium carbonate and cool the mixture			
e Use smaller lumps of calcium carbonate and add water to the acid			
f Use more concentrated acid and bigger lumps of calcium carbonate			

12 Write the letter of each reaction below one or more methods you could use to measure its rate.

A $Mg(s) + H_2SO_4(aq) \rightarrow MgSO_4(aq) + H_2(g)$

B $CaCO_3(s) + 2HNO_3(aq) \rightarrow Ca(NO_3)_2(aq) + CO_2(g) + H_2O(l)$

C $Na_2S_2O_3(aq) + 2HCl(aq) \rightarrow NaCl(aq) + SO_2(aq) + H_2O(l) + S(s)$

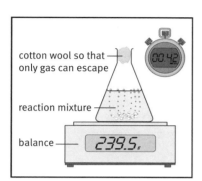
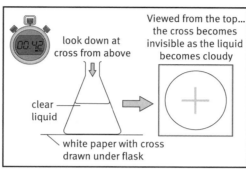
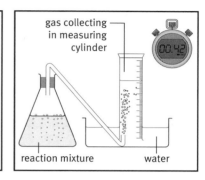

_____   _____   _____

13 Calculate the relative formula masses of the compounds below. Use the periodic table on page 31 to find the data you need.

a **i**   HCl _____

   ii $MgCO_3$ _____

   iii $MgCl_2$ _____

   iv CO_2 _____

   v H_2O _____

b Underneath the equation below, write

   ▸ the relative formula mass of each reactant and product
   ▸ the relative reacting mass of each reactant and product
   ▸ the reacting mass in grams of each reactant and product

$$2HCl + MgCO_3 \rightarrow MgCl_2 + CO_2 + H_2O$$

relative formula mass   ____   ____   ____   ____   ____

relative reacting mass   ____   ____   ____   ____   ____

reacting mass in g   ____   ____   ____   ____   ____

c Calculate the maximum mass of magnesium chloride you could make if you started with 42 g of magnesium carbonate.

Answer = _____ g

14 The table shows the actual and theoretical yields of three products.

Calculate the percentage yield for each product.

Formula of product	Actual yield	Theoretical yield	Working	Percentage yield
SrO	98 kg	104 kg		
Al_2O_3	222 g	224 g		
SF_6	68 t	73 t		

15 Solve the clues to fill in the grid.

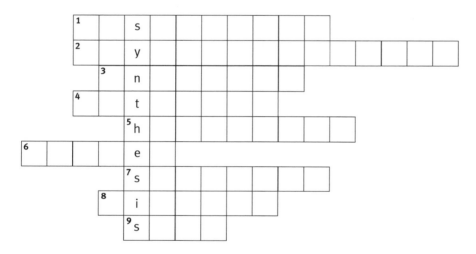

1 Use a _____ to finish drying a crystalline product of a synthesis.

2 Obtain a solid product from its solution by _____.

3 The point in a titration at which the reaction is just complete.

4 A chemical that speeds up a chemical reaction but is not used up in the process.

5 Alkaline solutions contain _____ ions.

6 Use more dilute solutions to make a reaction go _____.

7 React _____ acid with magnesium ribbon to make magnesium sulfate.

8 React nitric acid with calcium carbonate to make calcium _____.

9 A _____ is an ionic compound formed when an acid neutralizes an alkali.

Why is chemical synthesis important?

Chemical synthesis provides important chemicals for

- food additives
- fertilizers
- dyes
- paints
- pharmaceuticals (medicines)

Bulk chemicals are made on a huge scale – for example ammonia, sodium hydroxide, sulfuric acid, and chlorine.

Chemists synthesize small quantities of **fine chemicals**. These include drugs, pesticides, and chemicals needed by other manufacturers.

Chemical formulae

The table below shows the formulae of some important chemicals.

Name	Formula
chlorine	Cl_2
hydrogen	H_2
nitrogen	N_2
oxygen	O_2
hydrochloric acid	HCl
nitric acid	HNO_3
sulfuric acid	H_2SO_4
sodium hydroxide	NaOH
sodium chloride	NaCl

Name	Formula
sodium carbonate	Na_2CO_3
potassium chloride	KCl
magnesium oxide	MgO
magnesium hydroxide	$Mg(OH)_2$
magnesium carbonate	$MgCO_3$
magnesium sulfate	$MgSO_4$
calcium carbonate	$CaCO_3$
calcium chloride	$CaCl_2$

H The table below shows the formulae of some important ions.

Charge on ion	−2	−1	+1	+2
Examples	SO_4^{2-}	NO_3^-	H^+	Mg^{2+}
	CO_3^{2-}	Cl^-	Na^+	Ca^{2+}
		OH^-	K^+	

You can work out the **formula of an ionic compound** if you know the charges on its ions.

You can work out the **charge on an ion** if you know the formula of a salt that contains it and the charge on the other ion in the salt.

Page 36 shows how to do these calculations.

Relative atomic mass

The **relative atomic mass** is the mass of an atom of an element compared to the mass of an atom of carbon.

For example:

▶ The relative atomic mass of carbon is 12.
▶ The relative atomic mass of helium is 4.
▶ An atom of carbon is 3 times heavier than an atom of helium.

The periodic table shows the relative atomic mass of every element. (See page 31.)

Acids, alkalis, and indicators

An **acid** is a compound that dissolves in water to give a solution of pH less than 7. Acids produce aqueous hydrogen ions, $H^+(aq)$, in water.

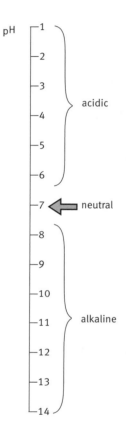

Pure acidic compounds include

▶ solids, for example citric acid and tartaric acid
▶ liquids, for example sulfuric acid, nitric acid, and ethanoic acid
▶ gases, for example hydrogen chloride

An **alkali** is a compound that dissolves in water to give a solution of pH greater than 7. Alkalis produce aqueous hydroxide ions, $OH^-(aq)$, in water.

Alkalis include potassium hydroxide, sodium hydroxide, and calcium hydroxide.

Indicators show whether a solution is acidic, alkaline, or neutral.

▶ Litmus is red in acid and blue in alkali.
▶ The range of colours of universal indicator show the pH of a solution.

pH meters also measure pH.

Acid reactions

Acids make **salts** in most of their reactions. Salts are ionic compounds.

▶ An acid reacts with a metal to make a salt and hydrogen.

$$\textbf{acid} + \textbf{metal} \rightarrow \textbf{salt} + \textbf{hydrogen}$$

For example:

hydrochloric acid + calcium → calcium chloride + hydrogen

$$HCl(aq) \quad + \quad Ca(s) \quad \rightarrow \quad CaCl_2(aq) \quad + \quad H_2(g)$$

▸ An acid reacts with a metal oxide to make a salt and water.

$$\textbf{acid} + \textbf{metal oxide} \rightarrow \textbf{salt} + \textbf{water}$$

For example:

sulfuric acid + magnesium oxide → magnesium sulfate + water

$$H_2SO_4(aq) \ + \quad MgO(s) \quad \rightarrow \quad MgSO_4(aq) \quad + H_2O(l)$$

▸ An acid reacts with a carbonate to make a salt, water and carbon dioxide.

$$\textbf{acid} + \textbf{metal carbonate} \rightarrow \textbf{salt} + \textbf{carbon dioxide} + \textbf{water}$$

For example:

sulfuric acid + magnesium carbonate → magnesium sulfate + carbon dioxide + water

$$H_2SO_4(aq) \ + \quad MgCO_3(s) \quad \rightarrow \quad MgSO_4(aq) \quad + \quad CO_2(g) \quad + H_2O(l)$$

▸ An acid reacts with a soluble metal hydroxide (alkali) to make a salt and water.

$$\textbf{acid} + \textbf{metal hydroxide} \rightarrow \textbf{salt} + \textbf{water}$$

For example:

hydrochloric acid + sodium hydroxide → sodium chloride + water

$$HCl(aq) \quad + \quad NaOH(aq) \quad \rightarrow \quad NaCl(aq) \quad + H_2O(l)$$

This is a **neutralization** reaction. Hydrogen ions from the acid react with hydroxide ions from the alkali to make water molecules:

$$H^+(aq) + OH^-(aq) \rightarrow H_2O(l)$$

Working out the formulae of salts

If you know the formulae of the acid and alkali that react together to make a salt, you can calculate the salt's formula.

Nitric acid (HNO_3) reacts with sodium hydroxide (NaOH) to make sodium nitrate. What is the formula of sodium nitrate?

▸ The charge on a hydroxide ion is −1. So the charge on a sodium ion is +1.
▸ The charge on a hydrogen ion is +1. So the charge on a nitrate ion is −1.

The total charge of the two ions in the formula of sodium nitrate must be zero.
So the formula shows one Na^+ ion and one NO_3^- ion. The formula is $NaNO_3$.

🄷 Balancing equations

Page 36 shows how to balance equations.

Planning and doing a chemical synthesis

Choose the reaction to make the product

You need to make calcium chloride. You could make it by reacting hydrochloric acid with calcium metal *or* calcium oxide *or* calcium carbonate. Calcium carbonate is the cheapest. So use the reaction:

calcium carbonate + hydrochloric acid → calcium chloride + carbon dioxide + water

Do a risk assessment

▶ Identify hazardous chemicals – dilute hydrochloric acid is an irritant. You will need to wear eye protection and keep it off your skin.

▶ Identify other hazards – carbon dioxide gas is produced. Make sure it can escape from the apparatus.

Work out the amounts of reactants to use

Add calcium carbonate to dilute hydrochloric acid.
Use excess calcium carbonate to make sure all the hydrochloric acid is used up.

▶ Calculate the relative formula masses of the reactants and of calcium chloride.
Page 89 shows how to do this.

▶ Calculate the relative reacting masses of the reactants and of calcium chloride. Take into account the numbers used to balance the equation.

▶ Add units to convert to reacting masses.

	$CaCO_3(s)$	+	$2HCl(aq)$	→	$CaCl_2(aq) + CO_2(g) + H_2O(l)$
Relative formula masses:	100		36.5		111
Reacting masses:	100 g		$(2 \times 36.5) = 71$ g		111 g

▶ Scale the reacting masses up or down to calculate the amounts you need.

For example, to make 11.1 g of calcium carbonate you need $(71 \div 10) = 7.1$ g of hydrogen chloride. This is the mass in 50 cm³ of hydrochloric acid solution that has a concentration of 142 g/litre.

10 g of calcium carbonate reacts exactly with 7.1 g of hydrochloric acid. You need excess calcium carbonate – more than 10 g. So use about 12 g.

Do the reaction in suitable apparatus in the right conditions

▶ Do the reaction in a beaker so the carbon dioxide gas can escape easily.

▶ Stir with a glass rod so the reactants mix well.

▶ Use small lumps of calcium carbonate – powder reacts too fast at room temperature.

▶ The excess calcium carbonate does not dissolve.

Separate the product from the reaction mixture

▶ Use **filtration** to separate the excess solid calcium carbonate from the product (calcium chloride solution) you have made.

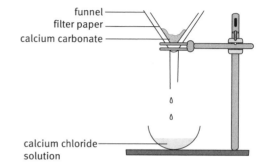

Purify the product

▶ Heat gently to **evaporate** some water.

▶ Leave the solution in an open Petri dish. Crystals form as more water evaporates. This is **crystallization**.

▶ Put the calcium chloride crystals in a dessicator to finish **drying**.

Measure the yield of the product

▶ Use a balance to measure the mass of dry calcium chloride crystals. This is the **actual yield**.

▶ Starting with 7.1 g of hydrogen chloride, the maximum possible yield of calcium chloride is 11.1 g. This is the **theoretical yield**.

▶ Calculate the percentage yield like this:

$$\text{percentage yield} = \frac{\text{actual yield}}{\text{theoretical yield}} \times 100\,\%$$

Checking the purity of a product

To check the purity of solid citric acid:

▶ Fill a burette with sodium hydroxide solution.

Make sure you know its exact concentration.

▶ Accurately weigh a sample of the solid citric acid.

Put it in a conical flask.

▶ Add pure water to the solid.

Stir until it dissolves.

▶ Add a few drops of phenolphthalein indicator.

This is colourless in acid solution.

▶ Add sodium hydroxide solution from the burette.

Stop adding it when one drop of sodium hydroxide solution makes the indicator go pink.

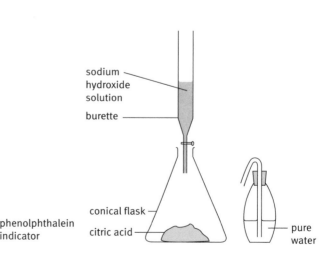

Reaction rates

The **rate of a reaction** is a measure of how quickly it happens.
Chemists control reaction rates so that a reaction is not dangerously fast
or uneconomically slow.

Measuring reaction rate

Methods for measuring reaction rate include:

▶ collecting a gas product and recording
its volume regularly

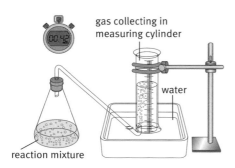

▶ measuring mass decrease as a gas
forms and recording the mass regularly

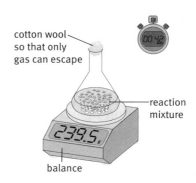

▶ measuring the time for a known
mass of solid to disappear

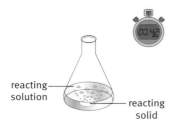

Mix the solid and liquid in the flask
and start the timer. Stop it when
you can no longer see any solid.

▶ measuring the time for a precipitate
to form

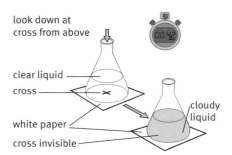

This is for reactions that produce an insoluble solid. Mix the
liquids in the flask and start the time. Stop it when you can no
longer see the cross on the paper through the solution.

Factors affecting reaction rate

These factors affect the rate of a reaction:

▶ The **concentration** of reactants in
solution – more concentrated solutions
react faster.

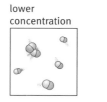

Ⓗ Molecules have a greater chance of colliding in a more
concentrated solution. More collisions means more reaction.
Reactions get faster if the reactants are more concentrated.

▶ **Temperature** – increasing the
temperature increases reaction rate.

▶ **Surface area** – 10 g of a powdered solid
has a bigger surface area than 10 g of one
lump of the same chemical. Increasing
surface area increases reaction rate.

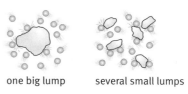

Ⓗ There is more contact between the solid
and the solution when there are several
small lumps. So the reaction is faster.

▶ A **catalyst** speeds up a reaction. It is not
used up in the chemical change.

1 a The names and formulae of some chemicals are given below.

Draw lines to match each formula to the correct name.

Formula
H_2SO_4
NaOH
NaCl
Na_2CO_3

Name
sodium carbonate
sodium chloride
sodium hydroxide
sulfuric acid

[3]

b i What is the state of pure ethanoic acid at room temperature?

Draw a (ring) around the correct answer.

solid **liquid** **gas** [1]

ii These are the hazard warning symbols on a container of pure ethanoic acid.

What do they tell you about ethanoic acid? Tick the correct answer.

It is corrosive and toxic. ☐

It is harmful and highly flammable. ☐

It is corrosive and harmful. ☐

It is highly flammable and an irritant ☐ [1]

c Some uses and purities of sodium chloride are shown below.

Draw lines to match each use with the correct purity.

Use
flavouring food
mixing with grit to put on icy roads
in a saline drip for a hospital patient

Purity
99.99 %
99.0 %
90.0 %

[2]

Total [7]

2 Dilute hydrochloric acid reacts with solid calcium carbonate to form a salt, water, and carbon dioxide gas.

a i Complete the equation to show

  ▸ the **formula of the salt** that is formed

  ▸ the **state symbol** for each of the chemicals at room temperature

  $2HCl$ —— $+ CaCO_3(s) →$ —————— $(aq) + CO_2$ —— $+ H_2O$ —— [3]

  ii In this reaction, what happens to the pH of the solution?

  Draw a (ring) around the best answer.

  goes up   **goes down**   **stays the same** [1]

b Yaasmeen carries out an experiment.

She sets up the apparatus below.

She reacts dilute hydrochloric acid with small lumps of calcium carbonate.

The calcium carbonate is present in excess.

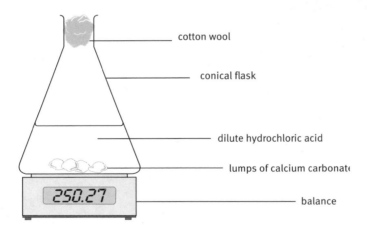

cotton wool

conical flask

dilute hydrochloric acid

lumps of calcium carbonate

balance

250.27

  i What happens to the reading on the balance as the reaction proceeds?

  ▸ Draw a (ring) around the best answer.

    increases   **decreases**

  ▸ Give a reason for your choice.

  _____

  _____ [1]

ii Yaasmeen repeats the experiment with hydrochloric acid of different concentrations.

She uses the same volume of hydrochloric acid.
She uses the same mass of the same type of calcium carbonate.
She does all the experiments at the same temperature.

This table shows Yaasmeen's results.

Concentration of acid (mol per dm³)	Time for mass to change by 0.2 g (minutes)
1.0	4.5
2.0	3.0
3.0	2.0

What happens to the rate of the reaction as Yaasmeen uses more concentrated acid?

▶ Draw a (ring) around the best answer.

   it gets faster   **it gets slower**   [1]

▶ Use the collision theory to explain why the rate of the reaction changes in this way.

   _____

   _____

   _____   [1]

iii Yaasmeen wants to make the reaction go **slower**.

What changes can she make?

Tick **two** boxes to show the correct answers.

   Do the reaction at a lower temperature.   ☐

   Stir the mixture in the flask.   ☐

   Use bigger lumps of calcium carbonate.   ☐

   Put a small piece of cotton wool in the top of the flask.   ☐   [2]

Total [9]

3 a Raj wants to know the purity of a sample of citric acid.
He does a titration to find out.
He uses this apparatus.

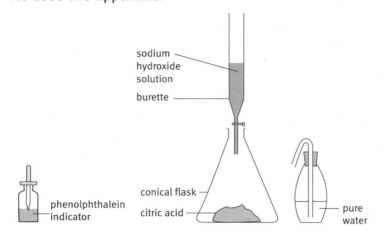

The stages below describe how Raj does the titration.

They are in the wrong order.

A Accurately weigh out a sample of citric acid. Put it in the conical flask.

B Add sodium hydroxide solution from the burette, a few cubic centimetres at a time. Swirl after each addition.

C Add sodium hydroxide solution from the burette, drop by drop. Swirl after each addition.

D Add a few drops of phenolphthalein indicator. This is colourless in acid solution.

E Stop adding sodium hydroxide solution when the indicator is permanently pink.

F Add pure water. Stir until the solid dissolves.

Fill in the boxes to show the correct order.
The first one has been done for you.

| A | | | | | |

[3]

b The reaction in the titration is a neutralization reaction.

  i Complete the word equation for the reaction.

  citric acid + sodium hydroxide → sodium citrate + _____ [1]

  ii The reaction can be represented by an **ionic equation**.

  Complete the ionic equation.

  H^+ + _____ → _____ [2]

  iii Give the name of the chemical that supplied the H^+ ions.

  _____ [1]

Total [7]

H 4 A company extracts mercury from its ore, mercury sulfide, by heating the ore in air.

This is the equation for the reaction.

$$HgS(s) + O_2(g) \rightarrow SO_2(g) + Hg(l)$$

a Calculate the maximum mass of mercury that can be extracted from 233 kg of mercury sulfide.

Answer = _____ kg   [2]

b In 2006, the company produced 1005 kg of mercury.

What mass of sulfur dioxide gas did the company produce as a by-product?

Answer = _____ kg   [2]

c Sulfur dioxide can be used to make sulfuric acid.

This is a simplified summary of the process:

$$SO_2 + \tfrac{1}{2}O_2 \rightarrow SO_3$$
$$SO_3 + H_2O \rightarrow H_2SO_4$$

How much sulfuric acid could the company make from the sulfur dioxide produced in **b**?

Answer = _____ kg   [2]

Total [6]

5 Grace wants to make copper sulfate crystals.

She reacts excess copper oxide powder with dilute sulfuric acid.

Below are the word and symbol equations for the reaction.

copper oxide + sulfuric acid → copper sulfate + water

$CuO(s)$ $+ H_2SO_4(aq)$ → $CuSO_4(aq)$ $+ H_2O(l)$

a Some of the stages of the process and the reason for each stage are shown below.

Draw lines to match each stage with the correct reason.

Stage		Reason
Stir the mixture of copper oxide and sulfuric acid.		To evaporate the rest of the water from the copper sulfate solution and to give the crystals time to form.
Filter the mixture.		To make sure the reactants mix together well.
Heat the filtrate over a Bunsen burner.		To separate the solution of copper sulfate from the excess copper oxide powder.
Let the filtrate cool. Leave it in an open Petri dish for a few days.		To evaporate most of the water from the copper sulfate solution.

[3]

b Grace calculates the theoretical yield of copper sulfate crystals from her reaction mixture. It is 4.0 g.

She actually makes 3.2 g of the crystals.

Calculate the percentage yield.

Answer = _____ kg   [1]

Total [4]

1   Draw lines to match each type of wave to

▶   the direction of vibrations
▶   one or more examples

Direction of vibrations
vibrations are at right angles to the direction in which the wave is moving
vibrations are in the same direction as the moving wave

Type of wave
longitudinal
transverse

Examples
X-rays
sound waves
water waves
waves on a rope

2   Fill in the empty boxes.

Word	Definition
wave	
	The material that a wave travels through.
frequency	
	This vibrates to make a wave.

3   Draw and label two arrows on the diagram to show the wave's **wavelength** and **amplitude**.

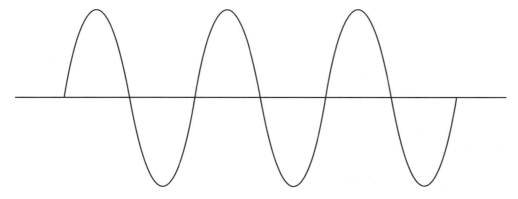

4   Calculate the speed of these waves. Include units in your answers.

a   A sound wave from a firework that travels 100 m in 0.3 seconds.

Answer = _____

b   A microwave that takes 0.000 033 3 seconds to travel from one mobile phone mast to another 10 km away.

Answer = _____

5 The diagrams represent water waves.

Write one word under each diagram. Choose from these words.

| reflection | digital | refraction | diffraction | interference | dispersion |

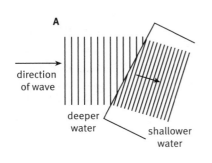

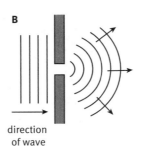

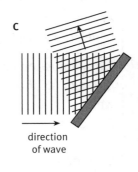

_____   _____   _____

6 Calculate the speed of these waves. Include units in your answers.

a Water waves in a swimming pool that are generated by a wave machine that vibrates once every second to produce waves of wavelength 2 m.

Answer = _____

b A sound wave from a bass guitar that has a frequency of 54 Hz and a wavelength of 6.3 m.

Answer = _____

7 Draw a ⟨ring⟩ round the correct bold words.

When two waves of the same frequency meet,
the effects of the waves add.

▶ If two waves arrive in step, they **reinforce / cancel out.**

This is **destructive / constructive** interference.

It is shown in diagram **A / B**.

▶ If two waves arrive out of step, they **reinforce / cancel out.**

This is **destructive / constructive** interference.

It is shown in diagram **A / B**.

A

B

H **8** Electromagnetic waves travel at about 300 000 000 m/s through space.

   a Hannah wants to listen to a radio station that transmits 200 000 Hz.

   What wavelength must she tune her radio to?

   Answer = _____

   b A TV satellite relays electromagnetic waves with a frequency of 500 million Hz.

   What is the wavelength of the waves?

   Answer = _____

9 Use these words to fill in the gaps.

speed	slower	faster	wavelength	amplitude	refraction
frequency	reflection	away from	towards	diffraction	

Once a source has made a wave, the wave's _____ cannot

change. When a wave goes from one medium to another,

its _____ and _____ change. The wave

then changes direction. This is called _____. Light

travels _____ in air than in water. So when a light ray

travels from air to water it bends _____ the normal.

10 Add beams of light to the diagrams to show:

   a Total internal reflection

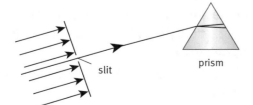

glass fibre

   b Refraction

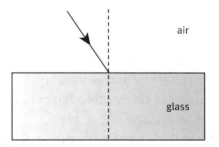

air

glass

   c Dispersion

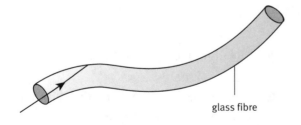

slit

prism

   d Reflection

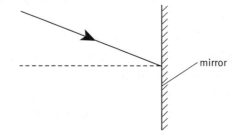

mirror

153

H **11** Complete the salesperson's speech bubble.

12 Solve the clues to fill in the grid.

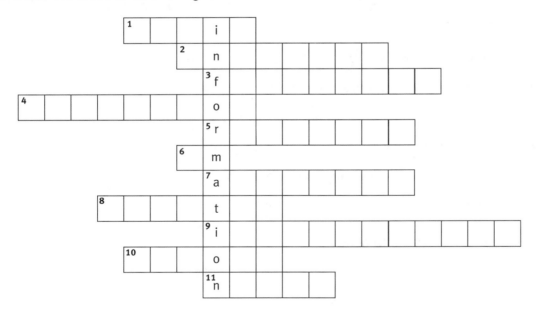

1 Signals are carried through space and the Earth's atmosphere by microwaves and _____ waves.

2 Signals are carried through optical fibres by light waves and _____ rays.

3 Waves that carry information must vary in amplitude or _____.

4 Information is carried by the pattern of a radio wave's _____.

5 A radio _____ decodes a radio wave's pattern of variation to reproduce the original sound.

6 The signal carried by FM and _____ radio waves varies in exactly the same way as the information from the original sound wave.

7 The signal carried by FM waves is called an _____ signal.

8 Sound waves can be converted into a _____ code made of two signals.

9 Analogue and digital signals pick up random unwanted signals as they travel. This is called _____, or noise.

10 Digital radio receivers pick up pulses and _____ them to make a copy of the original sound wave.

11 Digital radio receivers clean up signals to remove _____.

What are waves?

A wave is a disturbance that transfers energy in the direction the wave travels. Waves do not transfer matter. A wave comes from a source that **vibrates**. The material that a wave travels through is called the **medium**.

In a **transverse** wave, the particles vibrate at right angles to the direction of the wave's movement. Water waves are transverse.

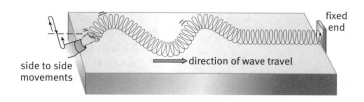

A transverse wave on a slinky spring

In a **longitudinal** wave, the particles vibrate in the same direction as the moving wave. Sound waves are longitudinal.

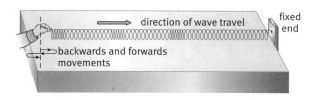

A longitudinal wave on a slinky spring

Describing waves

Frequency is the number of waves that the source makes every second. Its units are **hertz (Hz)**.

The diagram shows a wave's **wavelength** and **amplitude**.

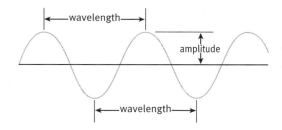

This equation gives the speed of a wave:

wave speed	=	**frequency**	×	**wavelength**
(metre per second, m/s)		(hertz, Hz)		(metre, m)

The frequency and speed of a wave are two separate things. For example, the speed of light in a vacuum is always the same, whatever the frequency of the wave.

Wave properties

Reflection

When waves are reflected, the angle of incidence equals the angle of reflection.

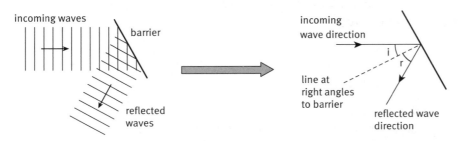

Reflection of water waves at a plane barrier. The angle of reflection (*r*) is equal to the angle of incidence (*i*).

Refraction

The speed of a wave depends on the medium. If a wave travels from one medium to another, its speed changes.

Once a vibrating source has made a wave, the wave's frequency cannot change. So when a wave's speed changes, its wavelength also changes. It may then change direction. This is **refraction**. The more the speed changes, the greater the direction change.

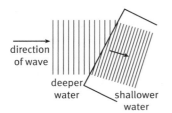

Refraction of water waves at a boundary between deep and shallow regions.

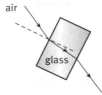

Refraction of a light ray when it enters and leaves a glass block.

Light waves travel faster in air than in glass. Imagine a light ray travelling through a glass block. It hits the glass–air boundary at an angle. If the angle of refraction for this ray would be greater than 90°, the ray is reflected. This is **total internal reflection**.

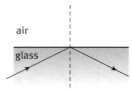

Light rays travel through optical fibres by total internal reflection. Optical fibres transmit telephone conversations. Doctors use optical fibre bundles to see inside bodies without cutting them open.

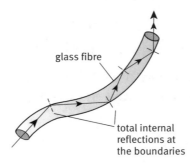

Diffraction

When waves go through a narrow gap, they bend and spread out. This is **diffraction**. The width of the gap must be similar to the wave's wavelength.

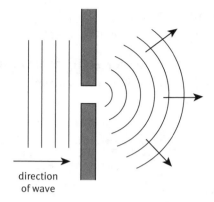

direction of wave

Interference

When two waves of the same frequency meet, the effects of the waves add. This is **interference**.

▶ If two waves arrive in step, they **reinforce**. This is **constructive interference**.

▶ If two waves arrive out of step, they **cancel out**. This is **destructive interference**.

Two light beams of the same frequency interfere. They make a pattern of dark and bright patches. The dark patches are where the two waves have cancelled each other out. The bright patches are the result of constructive interference.

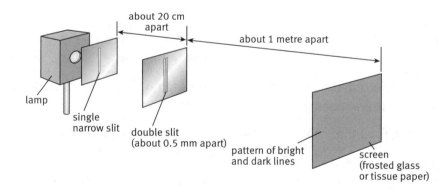

about 20 cm apart

about 1 metre apart

lamp

single narrow slit

double slit (about 0.5 mm apart)

pattern of bright and dark lines

screen (frosted glass or tissue paper)

Young's experiment. The double slits are two sources of light of the same frequency. Light from these interferes to produce a pattern on the screen.

Evidence for the wave nature of light

For many years, scientists were not sure how to think about light. Some scientists thought light rays were streams of tiny particles. Others believed light rays were waves. Evidence for the wave nature of light includes:

▶ Light rays **interfere**. They could not do this if they were a stream of tiny particles.

▶ Light rays can be **diffracted**.

Electromagnetic radiation

Electromagnetic waves consist of vibrating electric and magnetic fields.

Visible light is part of the **electromagnetic spectrum**. Different colours of light have different frequencies. The diagram shows the whole range of electromagnetic waves.

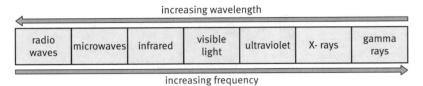

All electromagnetic waves have these properties:

▸ They can travel through space. Space contains no matter. It is a vacuum.

▸ They all travel through space at the same, very fast, speed.

Electromagnetic waves transfer energy. The energy is emitted or absorbed in 'packets', called **photons**.

The photons of high frequency waves carry more energy than the photons of low frequency waves.

The **intensity** of a beam of electromagnetic radiation is the energy it delivers every second. Intensity depends on

▸ the number of photons that arrive each second and

H ▸ the amount of energy that each photon carries

Different frequencies of electromagnetic waves have different uses.

Type of wave	Use	Why the waves can be used in this way
radio waves	carrying information for radio and TV programmes	they are not strongly absorbed by the atmosphere
microwaves	heating food that contains water	they are strongly absorbed by water molecules
	carrying information between communications satellites and metal satellite dishes	they are reflected by metals they are not strongly absorbed by the atmosphere
light and infrared radiation	carrying information along optical fibres	they lose only very little energy when travelling through optical fibres
X-rays	taking 'shadow' pictures of bones or luggage	they are absorbed by dense materials, but not as much by less dense ones

Adding information to waves

Radio, TV, and telephone systems transmit information over long distances. Their signals can be carried by

▸ radio waves and microwaves through space and the Earth's atmosphere

▸ light waves and infrared rays through optical fibres

Analogue signals

The waves that carry information must be made to vary in amplitude or frequency. The pattern of variation carries the information.

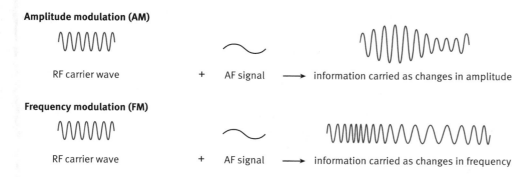

Amplitude modulation (AM)

RF carrier wave   +   AF signal   ⟶   information carried as changes in amplitude

Frequency modulation (FM)

RF carrier wave   +   AF signal   ⟶   information carried as changes in frequency

Radio waves travel through the atmosphere to a radio **receiver**. The receiver decodes the pattern of variation. It reproduces the original sound.

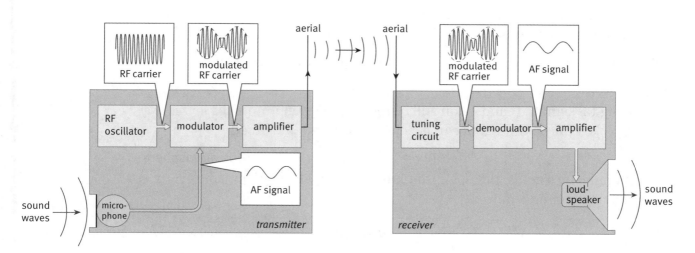

A simple radio system. When you speak into the microphone, a copy of the sound comes out of the loudspeaker. (RF is the radio frequency; AF is the audio frequency.)

The signal carried by AM and FM radio waves varies in exactly the same way as the information from the original sound wave. It is called an **analogue signal**.

Digital signals

Information is transmitted **digitally** like this:

◗ Sound waves are converted into a **digital code** consisting of two values (0 and 1).

◗ The digital code is transmitted as short bursts of waves, called pulses (0 = no pulse; 1 = pulse).

◗ Radio receivers pick up the pulses. They **decode** the pulses to make a copy of the original sound wave.

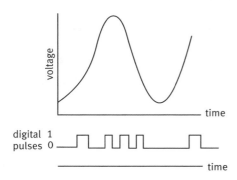

An analogue system and its corresponding digital pulses

Analogue and digital: which is better?

As analogue and digital signals travel, they pick up random unwanted electrical signals. This is **noise**, or interference.

Analogue and digital signals decrease in intensity as their amplitudes get smaller. So radio receivers must **amplify** the signals they receive – including any noise that has been added to the signal.

Digital signals transmit information with higher quality than analogue signals because

◗ with digital signals, 0 and 1 can still be recognized even if noise has been picked up. So the signal can be 'cleaned up' by removing the noise

◗ with analogue signals, the noise that has been amplified by the radio receiver cannot be removed

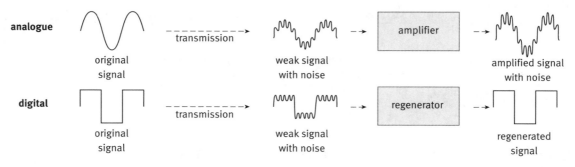

Digital signals can be 'cleaned up' by regenerators, but when analogue signals are amplified, noise gets amplified as well.

1 A new device helps hostage negotiators to track people's movements inside a room.

▶ The device sends radar pulses through the wall and into the room.

▶ Furniture and people reflect the radar.

▶ The device detects the reflected signals and analyses them.

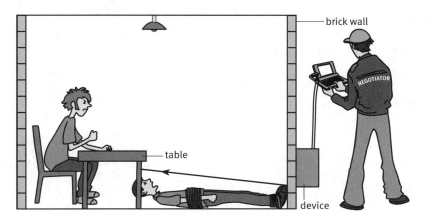

a Use a ruler to draw an arrow on the diagram to show the direction of the radar pulse after it has been reflected by the table leg. [1]

b Radar pulses are microwaves.

The diagram shows the electromagnetic spectrum.

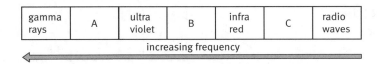

gamma rays	A	ultra violet	B	infra red	C	radio waves

increasing frequency

Which letter (A,B or C) represents microwaves? _____ [1]

c The device emits microwaves with a wavelength of 0.03 m.

Microwaves travel through air with a speed of 300 000 000 m/s.

Calculate the frequency of the microwaves.

Answer = _____ Hz [2]

d The device does not work if the wall is made from metal.

Explain why.

_____

_____ [1]

Total [5]

2 There was an earthquake under the sea. Big waves moved through the sea, away from the centre of the earthquake. The waves were a tsunami. The tsunami caused great damage when it arrived at land.

a Scientists measured the tsunami waves as they arrived at a beach.

They made notes and drew a diagram.

Write down the amplitude, wavelength, and frequency of the waves.

Include units in your answers.

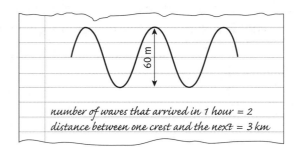

number of waves that arrived in 1 hour = 2
distance between one crest and the next = 3 km

▶ Amplitude = _____

▶ Frequency = _____

▶ Wavelength = _____ [3]

b The tsunami waves arrived at a big bay.

The entrance to the bay is 50 km wide.

The waves bent when they enter the bay.

i Draw on the diagram to show two waves in the bay. [1]

ii Give the name of the effect that happens at the harbour mouth.

_____

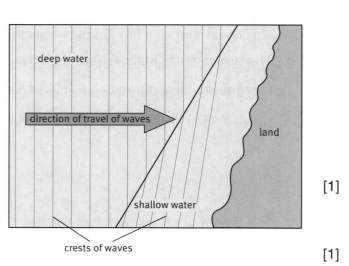

entrance to bay — bay land

crests of 3 waves [1]

c Near one coastline, the tsunami moved from deep water to shallow water.

The waves changed direction.

A scientist drew this diagram to show the crests of the waves.

i What is this effect called?

_____ [1]

ii Draw an arrow on the diagram to show the direction of travel of the waves in the shallow water.

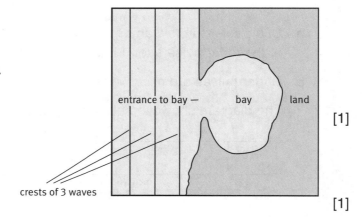

deep water

direction of travel of waves

land

shallow water

crests of waves [1]

Total [7]

3 a The diagrams show different types of radio signal.

Draw a line to match each diagram to its description.

Diagram

Type of signal
frequency modulated (FM)
amplitude modulated (AM)
digital

[3]

b The stages below show how radio programmes are transmitted and received digitally. They are in the wrong order.

A A radio receiver converts the digital electrical signals into sound waves.

B Sound waves are converted into digital signals.

C A radio receiver converts radio waves to digital electrical signals.

D Radio waves travel through the atmosphere.

E The digital signals are transmitted as a series of pulses.

Fill in the boxes to show the correct order.

☐ ☐ ☐ ☐ ☐

[4]

c Explain why digital signals transmit information with higher quality than analogue signals.

_____

_____

_____

_____

[2]

Total [9]

4

> Scientists have invented a scanner to find out if premature babies are at risk of brain damage.
>
> The scanner sends beams of light into the brain.
> It uses light of two wavelengths: 780 nm and 815 nm.
>
> Some of the light passes through brain tissue.
> Some of the light is absorbed by water in the brain.
> Most of the light is scattered in all directions.
>
> Detectors in the scanner measure the intensity of the light that comes out of the brain. If the intensity is less than expected, the baby's brain might be bleeding.
>
> The scanner builds up a 3-dimensional image of the brain.
> Doctors can use this to find out where the bleeding is.

a What scientific word means that light **passes through** brain tissue?

Draw a (ring) around the correct answer.

transmitted   **reflected**   **absorbed**   [1]

b Use the information in the box to decide whether blood transmits, reflects, or absorbs the light that the scanner emits.

Draw a (ring) around the correct answer.

transmits   **reflects**   **absorbs**   [1]

Give a reason for your decision.

One mark is for writing in sentences with correct spelling, punctuation and grammar.

_____

_____

_____

_____   [2 + 1]

H

c The diagram shows some of the detectors around a baby's head.

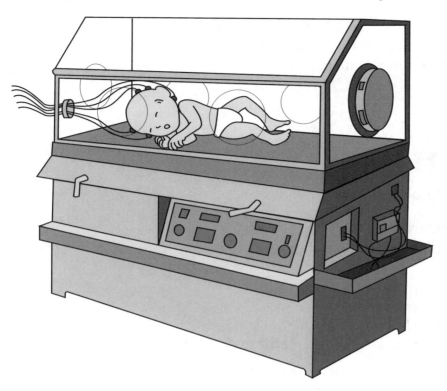

Each detector records a different reading for light intensity.

Why are the readings different?

Tick the **best** answer.

The amount of energy carried by a photon does not change. ☐

In one second, a different number of photons arrives at
each detector. ☐

The amount of energy carried by a photon changes each
second. ☐

Each photon carries the same amount of energy. ☐   [1]

d i Give one reason why it would not be sensible for the scanner to
send X-rays into the brain.

_____   [1]

ii Give one reason why it would not be sensible for the scanner to
send microwaves into the brain.

_____   [1]

Total [8]

Investigation

Your practical investigation counts for 33.3 % of your total grade. You will do the work in class. If you do more than one investigation, your teacher will choose the best one for your marks.

What you will do

In your investigation you will:

▶ choose a question to investigate
▶ select equipment and use it safely and appropriately
▶ make accurate and reliable observations

How your teacher will award marks

Your teacher will award marks under five headings.

Strategy

▶ Choose the task for your investigation.
▶ Decide how much data to collect.
▶ Choose equipment and techniques to give you precise and reliable data.

To get high marks here, choose a task which is not too simple. Plan to collect an appropriate range of precise and reliable data. Give reasons for your choice of equipment and techniques. Try to work as independently as possible.

Collecting data

▶ Work safely.
▶ Take careful and accurate measurements.
▶ Collect enough data and repeat it to check its reliability.
▶ Collect data across an appropriate range.
▶ Control other things that might affect your results.

To get high marks here, do preliminary work to decide the range. Collect data across the whole range. Repeat readings to make them as reliable as possible. Make sensible decisions about how to treat anomalous results (outliers). Use the apparatus skilfully to make precise readings. Try changing your techniques if you think that might give you better data.

Interpreting data

▶ Use charts, tables, diagrams, or graphs to show patterns in your results.
▶ Say what conclusions you can make from your data.
▶ Explain your conclusions using your science knowledge and understanding.

To get high marks here, label graph axes and table headings correctly. If appropriate, analyse your results mathematically. Summarize your evidence by identifying trends and correlations. Say whether there are any limitations in your data. Finally, use detailed scientific knowledge to explain your conclusion.

Evaluation

▶ Look back at your experiment and say how you could improve the method.
▶ Say how reliable you think your evidence is.
▶ Suggest improvements or extra data you could collect to be more confident in your conclusions.

To get high marks here, describe improvements to the method in detail. Say why they would be improvements. Use the pattern of your results, and the scatter between repeats, to help you to assess accuracy and reliability. Give reasons for any anomalous results. Say how confident you are in your conclusions, and give reasons for your decision. Describe in detail what extra data you would like to collect to make your conclusions more secure.

Presentation

▶ Write a full report of your investigation.
▶ Choose a sensible order for the different parts of your report, and lay it out clearly.
▶ Describe the apparatus you used and what you did with it.
▶ Show units correctly.
▶ Make sure your spelling, punctuation and grammar are accurate.
▶ Use scientific words when appropriate.

To get high marks here, state your investigation question clearly. Describe accurately and in detail how you did the practical work. Include all the data you collected, including repeat values. Make sure you record the data with appropriate accuracy and that you include all units. Record all your observations thoroughly and in detail.

Secondary data

As well as the data you collect, you may also use information from other people's work. This is secondary data. You can get secondary data from other students, the Internet, libraries, and textbooks. Or you might like to speak to a scientist or write to an organization. Think carefully about what you want to find out before looking for secondary data. This will help you to get the information you need without wasting time!

Answers to questions

B4 Workout

1 Vigorous exercise – temperature, hydration, salt levels, blood oxygen levels; living in hot climates – temperature, hydration, salt levels; scuba diving – blood oxygen levels; mountain climbing – blood oxygen levels

2 Receptor – to detect stimuli – temperature sensor; processing centre – to receive information and coordinate responses – thermostat with switch; effector – to produce the response – heater

3 Protein, speed up, 37, slow, there are few collisions between enzyme molecules and reacting molecules, denatured, because the shape of the active site changes, active site, lock and key

4 1F, 2C, 3G, 4B, 5F, 6A, 7D, 8E

5   2   Hot dry skin, fast pulse rate, dizzy and confused
    3   42
    4   When it is very hot you sweat more. This made you dehydrated. So you sweated less. So your body temperature rose out of control and your body's normal methods of temperature control stopped working.

6   2   Shivering, confusion, slurred speech, not co-ordinated
    3   Insulate him, warm him slowly with warm towels, give him a warm drink
    4   35 °C. His body lost energy faster than it gained energy.

7 **a** DO   **b** DO   **c** D   **d** D   **e** DO
   f D   **g** O   **h** A   **i** A

8 **a** Enters in food, drinks and as a result of respiration; leaves in sweating, breathing, faeces, urine
   b **i** ... the membrane may rupture
      ii ... solutions in the cell get too concentrated so the cell cannot work properly

9 CEADB

10 **a** T   **b** T   **c** T   **d** T   **e** F
    f F   **g** F   **h** T   **i** T   **j** F
    k F

11 1 A, 2 C, 3 D, 4 K, 5 E, 6 F, 7 B, 8 G, 9 H, 10 L, 11 I, 12 J

B4 GCSE-style questions

1 **a** Temperature sensor – skin; heater (switched on) – muscle cells (contracting quickly to cause shivering); thermostat with a switch – brain; heater (switched off) – sweat glands
   b **i** If there is a change in the system, there is an action that reverses the change.
      ii e.g. The response is very sensitive.

2 **a** Protein
   b **i** At 30 °C collisions between catalase and hydrogen peroxide are more frequent and have more energy.
      ii It has been denatured.
   c A
   d **i** Active site
      ii The shape of the active site is changed so reacting molecules no longer fit into the active site.

3 **a** Two from: hot dry skin, fast pulse rate, dizzy, confused
   b Sensors

   c You are less likely to get dehydrated so you can continue to sweat.
   d The brain and other organs return to normal temperature.
   e When sweat evaporates, energy is transferred from skin to sweat. This cools you down. If you do not sweat, your body's temperature rises out of control.
   f **i** Processing centre
      ii Alcohol results in big volumes of dilute urine, so less water is available to make sweat.
   g The body detects that it is losing too much heat. So it shuts down circulation to the skin. So all the hot blood in the skin is diverted towards the brain.

4 **a** Two from: water, carbon dioxide, oxygen
   b **i** Molecules move from a region of their high concentration to a region of their low concentration through a partially permeable membrane.
      ii The cell may rupture.
   c Na^+ ion – diffusion; K^+ ion – active transport; water molecule – osmosis

C4 Workout

1 **a** Column B: harmful, toxic, oxidizing
   b Column C: wash off spills quickly; use in a well ventilated room, wear gloves, use in fume cupboard or wear mask over nose and mouth; keep away from flammable chemicals

2 Life is fun. So is revision.

3 Picture of a snail

4 She is beautiful, I think.

5 Red – group 2, blue – period 3, non–metals see p.31, three from group 1, three from group 6

6 **a** 3   **b** N   **c** 4   **d** Fe   **e** N

7 **a** 7   **b** 1   **c** 7   **d** B   **e** 1
   f 7   **g** 1   **h** 7   **i** 1   **j** B
   k 7   **l** 7

8 **a** hydrogen   **b** potassium chloride   **c** iodine
   d water, hydrogen   **e** chlorine, sodium   **f** bromine

9 Missing names: potassium bromide, lithium iodide
   Missing formulae: H_2O, H_2, NaOH, Cl_2

10 **a** $2K(s) + 2H_2O(l) \rightarrow 2KOH(aq) + H_2(g)$
    b $2Na(s) + Cl_2(g) \rightarrow 2NaCl(s)$
    c $2Li(s) + 2H_2O(l) \rightarrow 2LiOH(aq) + H_2(g)$
    d $Cl_2(g) + 2K(aq) \rightarrow 2KCl(s)$
    e $2Fe(s) + 3Cl_2(g) \rightarrow 2FeCl_3$

11 Potassium and chlorine – Q; lithium and iodine – S

12

lithium   beryllium   carbon   fluorine

sodium   phosphorus   chlorine   argon

13 Nucleus, neutrons, shells, electrons, electrons, 7

14 Solid ionic compounds form crystals – their ions are arranged in a regular lattice; the charge on a sodium ion is +1 – because it is made when an atom loses an electron; the charge on a bromide ion is −1 – because it is made when an atom gains an electron; liquid ionic compounds conduct electricity – because their ions are free to move; ionic compounds conduct electricity when they are dissolved in water – because their ions are free to move; solid ionic compounds do not conduct electricity – because their ions are not free to move

15

Symbol of atom or ion	Cl	I⁻	K⁺	Li	Br⁻	Li⁺	Na
Number of protons	17	53	19	3	35	3	11
Number of electrons	17	54	18	3	36	2	11

16 a NaBr   **b** KCl   **c** MgS   **d** K_2O
e CaO   **f** $CaBr_2$

17 a +2   **b** +2   **c** +1   **d** +1

C4   GCSE–style questions

1 a Iodine is a grey solid at room temperature; chlorine is a gas at room temperature; chlorine is green.
b Iodine atom – I; iodine molecule – I_2; iodide ion – I⁻
c   **i** sodium + fluorine
    ii $2Na(s) + F_2(g) \longrightarrow 2NaF(s)$

2 a   **i** Toxic, corrosive
    ii One of: wear gloves; work in a fume cupboard; wear mask over nose and mouth.
b   **i**

Sodium	11	11	10	Na⁺
Fluorine / fluoride	9	9	10	F⁻

    ii

c The sodium and fluoride ions separate from each other and are free to move independently in the water.
d The sodium and fluoride ions are charged particles that are free to move independently.
e Sodium chloride and sodium fluoride are both white crystalline solids.

3 a 14   **b** Ar
c One from: sulfur, selenium, tellurium, polonium
d One from: sodium, aluminium, silicon, phosphorus, sulfur, chlorine, argon

4 a   **i** Tarnishes; lithium floats and fizzes gently; purple
    ii $2Li(s) + 2H_2O(l) \longrightarrow 2LiOH(aq) + H_2(g)$
b   **i** LiCl
    ii White crystalline solid
c Row 1 – Li_2CO_3; row 2 – O^{2-}; row 3 – lithium bromide, LiBr

5 a Mistakes: melting point of lithium; formula of caesium hydroxide; relative reactivity of potassium
b   **i** CsCl
    ii Two from: caesium melts, jumps from surface of water, flame
    iii Hydrogen and caesium hydroxide

6 a C, D   **b** B   **c** A, D   **d** C, D
e A   **f** C

P4   Workout

1 a B   **b** A   **c** B   **d** A

2 Rope 10 N to right; tricycle 120 N to right; trolley no resultant force

3 Picture 1 – C; picture 2 – B; picture 3 – A

4 a F   **b** T   **c** F   **d** F   **e** T
f F   **g** T

5 A B D E C

6 a T   **b** T   **c** T   **d** F   **e** T
f T   **g** F

7 a 200 m/min   **b** 40 m/s
c 18 m/s   **d** 4 cm/s

8 In order along the curve: B, A, C, E, D, F

9 a 0 km/h   **b** 7.5 km/h

10 a 88 000 kg m/s   **b** 304 kg m/s   **c** 13.5 kg m/s

11 In order along the curve: A, B, D, F, E, C

12 15 000 Ns

13 a 30 000 J   **b** 1 250 000 J   **c** 58 J

14 a 3 J   **b** 3 J   **c** 7.8 m/s

15 1 interaction, 2 kinetic, 3 tachographs, 4 resultant, 5 friction, 6 average, 7 reaction, 8 potential, 9 driving, 10 momentum, 11 negative

P4   GCSE-style questions

1 a   **i** D to E
    ii Stationary from B to C; moving at a steady speed from C to D – this is the fastest part of the fire engine's journey
    iii 1 km/min
b 12 m/s
c

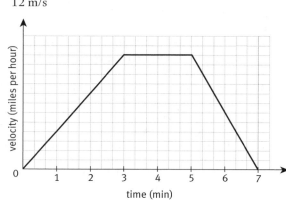

2 **a** Bottom row is correct
   b Increases
   c The counter–force and driving force are equal and opposite.

3 **a** **i** All statements are true except the first one
      ii 1500 J
      iii 1500 J
   b 300 J

4 **a** 16 200 kg m/s
   b 1 620 000 N
   c Seatbelts stretch during a collision; seatbelts reduce the force that the driver experiences; seatbelts make you move forward more slowly during a collision.

5 **a** 45 000 J
   b 45 000 J

B5 Workout

1 Chromosomes, genes, DNA, double helix, copied

2 Top row: A, D, H; bottom row: 1B, 2G, 3F, 4C, 5E

3 **1** testes, meiosis, 4, sperm; **2** 23; **3** ovaries, meiosis, 4, eggs; **4** 23; **5** fertilization; **6** zygote, 23, 46; **7** mitosis, 2, 46; **8** 2, 4; **9** 4, 8; **10** stem; **11** 16

4

	Meiosis	Mitosis
What does it make?	gametes (sex cells)	body cells
How many new cells does each parent cell make?	4	2
How many chromosomes are in each new cell?	half as many as in the parent cell	same as in parent cell
Where does it happen?	in sex organs	in body cells
Why does it happen?	to make sex cells for sexual reproduction	so an organism can grow, reproduce and replace damaged cells

5 Correct bold words: **a** weak, 2; **b** T, C; **c** 4; **d** 2
   Matching pairs: 1**c**, 2**a**, 3**b**, 4**d**

6 For example:
   1 Treating disease and replacing damaged tissues, for example growing skin cell to treat burns and growing nerve cells to treat spinal injuries.
   3 All their genes are still switched on – they can grow into any type of specialized cell.
   4 Patients must take drugs to stop their bodies rejecting the transplanted tissue.
   5 The genes of the new tissues are the same as the patient's.
   6 The genes are different to the patient's.
   7 Treat burns and spinal injuries.

7 Plants – A, C, G, I; animals – D, F; both – B, E, H

8 —

9 Auxin, chromosomes, double, embryonic, fetus, gametes, mitochondria, nucleus, organelles, phototropism, tissues, unspecialized, xylem, young, zygote

B5 GCSE-style questions

1 **a** Gametes, testes, 4, different, 15
   b **i** Egg or ovum
      ii Fertilization
   c C A D B

2 **a** **i** They can grow many plants quickly and cheaply; they can reproduce a plant with exactly the features they want.
      ii Auxins
      iii Meristem cells
      iv Leaves, flowers
   b **i** Plants need light energy for photosynthesis – the more light that falls on the leaf, the faster photosynthesis happens (up to a maximum speed).
      ii Phototropism
      iii B

3 **a** **i** Stem cells are unspecialized cells. They divide and develop into specialized cells.
      ii They will grow heart muscle cells from the stem cells.
   b **i** One of: embryos, adults
      ii One of: (embryos) ethical objections, problem of rejection; (adults) difficult to separate from other cells, problem of rejection

4 **a** Double helix
   b It gives instruction for joining amino acids in the correct order to make a certain protein.
   c B A D C

C5 Workout

1 Box 1: A, oxygen, argon, carbon dioxide, nitrogen
   Box 2: B, sodium chloride, potassium bromide, magnesium chloride
   Box 3: C, silicon dioxide, aluminium oxide
   Box 4: D, glucose, DNA

2 Ab1; Ad1; Ba2; Bh9; Bi10, Cc3, Ce6, Cf8, Ch4, Da5, Dc3, Dg7

3 From top to bottom: O_2, Ar, H_2O, CO_2

4 Nitrogen gas – simple covalent – −210; silicon dioxide – giant covalent – 1610; sodium chloride – giant ionic −801

5 **a** NaCl   **b** $MgCl_2$ **c** KBr   **d** $MgSO_4$

6 **a** Oxygen **b** nitrogen **c** oxygen **d** oxygen
   e aluminium

7 For example:
   2 Beautiful, rare and hard
   4 The covalent bonds between the atoms on the surface are very strong – it takes a lot of energy to break them. Trying to scratch the surface does not provide enough energy to do this.

8 Alanine – $C_3H_7O_2N$; threonine – $C_4H_8O_3N$; cysteine – $C_3H_7O_2NS$

9 **a** Equation already balanced; ZnO is reduced; C is oxidized

   b $Fe_2O_3 + 3C \rightarrow 2Fe + 3CO$; Fe_2O_3 is reduced; C is oxidized

10 **a** 130 tonnes   **b** 27 kg

11 A C B E D

12 1 DNA, 2 aluminium, 3 mineral, 4 lithosphere, 5 electrolysis, 6 salts, 7 sandstone, 8 electrostatic, 9 carbon, 10 nitrogen

C5   GCSE-style questions

1 **a** Molecular
   b 80 g
   c **i** Carbon, hydrogen, oxygen, nitrogen
      ii $C_3H_7O_3N$

2 **a** **i** Photosynthesis, combustion

      ii Weathering of exposed rocks, burial of shellfish
   b **i** O_2
      ii They have low melting points; they do not conduct electricity
   c **i** $2Fe_2O_3$ and $2H_4SiO_4$
      ii 224 kg

3 **a** **i** Hydrosphere
      ii When solid, it does not conduct electricity – The charged particles cannot move; It has a high melting point – There are strong attractive forces between the ions; When solid it forms crystals – The ions are arranged in a regular pattern; When liquid, it conducts electricity – The charged particles can move.
      iii $MgBr_2$
   b 76.9 m^3
   c **i** An electric current decomposes the electrolyte; an electric current passes through liquid magnesium chloride; chlorine gas is made.
      ii $Mg^{2+} + 2e^- \rightarrow Mg$

4 **a** Giant, strong
   b **i** C   **ii** E
   c Hard and attractive

P5   Workout

1 Electrons, negatively, negative, positive, attractive, repel

2 All conductors ... contain charges that are free to move; insulators ... do not conduct electricity; insulators ... include polythene, wood, and rubber; insulators ... do not contain charges that are free to move; metal conductors ... contain charges that are free to move; metal conductors ... contain electrons that are free to move; in a complete circuit charges are not used up; in a complete circuit ... the battery makes free charges flow in a continuous loop.

3 Hotter, moving, stationary, more, smaller

4 Ammeter (A); voltmeter (V); cell —|⊢—;

   power supply —|⊢—|⊢— (battery) or —+∘ ∘-— (DC)

   or —∘~∘— (AC); lamp ⊗; switch —∘ ∘—;

   LDR —▭—; fixed resistor —▭—;

   variable resistor —▱—; thermistor —▱—

5 **a** B   **b** A   **c** B

6 Circuit 1: B F H; circuit 2: A C D; both circuits: E G

7 **a** 14.23 Ω   **b** 30 Ω

8 **a** 0.4 A   **b** 3 V

9 Clockwise from top: the same as, volts, voltage, push, potential energy, less

10 **a** Both are 100 mA
   b **i** Resistor on right
      ii Greatest; ... more work is done by charge flowing through a large resistance than through a small one.
   c **i** 0.6 V
      ii ... the p.d.s across the components add up to the p.d. across the battery

11 Computer – energy transferred is 0.5 kWh
   Kettle – energy transferred is 0.09 kWh
   Toaster – power rating is 1 200 W or 1.2 kW
   Mobile phone charger – power rating is 0.02 kW

12 **a** £ 0.24   **b** £ 0.10

13 Coil, current, out, pole

14 **a** 3.91 A   **b** 0.870 A

15 11.5 V

16 1 resistance, 2 current, 3 kWh, 4 power, 5 V, 6 parallel, 7 voltmeter, 8 Ω, 9 generator, 10 induction, 11 R, 12 direct, 13 AC, 14 A, 15 efficiency, 16 DC

P5   GCSE-style questions

1 **a** When the switch is closed, the battery makes free charges in the circuit move; the metal wires contain electrons that are free to move; when the switch is closed there is a flow of charge.
   b Voltage, current, resistance, current, current, resistance

2 **a** **i** Voltmeter connected in parallel to the heater
      ii 1.2 Ω
   b Moving electrons bump into stationary atoms in the wire.

3 **a** 788 kWh
   b : 24
   c 245 hours

4 **a** **i** 230 V   **ii** 230 V
   b 3 amps
   c Stays the same
   d **i** 14.4 amps
      ii Fridge – current is smallest through this appliance whilst the voltage across all the appliances is the same.

5 **a** Increase the number of coils, increase the strength of the magnet, put an iron core inside the coil.
   b **i** Iron, induces
      ii 120

B6   Workout

1   Stimulus, response, behaviour

2   **a**   Grasping a finger or similar tightly in palm
    b   Sucking nipple in mouth
    c   Stepping when feet touch flat surface
    d   Startling (or Moro reflex) - spreading out arms and legs on hearing a loud noise

3   **a** S   **b** C   **c** S   **d** S   **e** C

4   Receptors: A B E F; effectors: C D G H

5   Left from top: motor neuron, sensory neuron, effector, receptor
    Right: spinal cord

6   A F C D E B

7   Nucleus – controls cell; cytoplasm – cell reactions happen here; cell membrane – substances get into and out of the cell through this; fatty sheath – insulates neuron from neighbouring cells; branched endings – make connections with other neurons or effectors.

8   Bird: Those caterpillars are poisonous. She won't eat them again because they taste so bad.
    Caterpillar: She's learnt that caterpillars like us don't taste good – so that's one less bird that's going to try to eat me.

9   From the top: The sensory neuron releases a chemical into the synapse and the chemical diffuses across the synapse; a nerve impulse gets to the end of the sensory neuron; the chemical arrives at receptor molecules on the motor neuron's membrane and the chemical's molecules bind to the receptor molecules. This stimulates a nerve impulse in the motor neuron.

10 Short-term memory A C; long-term memory B, D; both E

11 **a**   Consciousness, language, intelligence, memory
    b   ... studying patients with brain damage, electrically stimulating different parts of the brain, doing MRI scans.
    c   ... adapt to new situations and learn to interact effectively with others.
    d   Neurons, pathways

12 A F C E B D G H

13 Horizontal: 3 consciousness, 5 multi-store, 6 repetition, 7 shop, 8 muscle, 9 feral, 10 axon, 11 CNS, 12 cortex, 13 N, 14 pathways, 15 short-term, 16 model, 17 neuroscientist
    Vertical: 1 serotonin, 2 synapse, 3 cerebral, 4 neuron, 15 stimulus

B6   GCSE-style questions

1   **a**   Grips finger; spreads out arms and legs when she hears a sudden noise.
    b   ... something being put in her mouth; milk
    c   e.g. Cannot respond to new situations, so often fail to survive environmental changes

2   **a**   Effector cells – make changes in response to stimulus; receptor cells – detect a stimulus; brain and spinal cord – control response to stimulus
    b   **i**   (Left) sensory neuron, (right top) central nervous system), (right bottom) motor neuron
        ii   Electrical, peripheral central

3   **a**   A dolphin's brain has a great variety of potential neuron pathways.
    b   A C E D B F G

4   **a**   Stimulus, response, learned, conditioned
    b   **i**   The bitter taste means the insect may be poisonous. So the bird has avoided eating something poisonous.
        ii   Birds do not eat hover flies because they look as though they might have a bitter taste and therefore be poisonous.

5   **a**   A C E B F D
    b   Ecstasy causes an increase in the concentration of serotonin in the brain; Ecstasy blocks sites in the brain's synapses where serotonin is removed.

C6   Workout

1   Food additives, e.g. saccharin; pharmaceuticals, e.g. paracetamol; fertilizers, e.g. ammonium nitrate; plastics, e.g. polythene

2   **a**   pharmaceuticals
    b   11 %
    c   9.5 %

3   Names: magnesium sulfate, potassium chloride, sodium carbonate
    Formulae: N_2, HNO_3, $CaCl_2$, $CaCO_3$

4   Solids – tartaric, citric; liquids – sulfuric, ethanoic, nitric; gas – none

5   **a** acid **b** alkali **c** acid **d** alkali **e** both
    f alkali **g** both **h** acid **i** both

6   **a** +2   **b** +3

7   Formulae: KCl, Na_2SO_4, $Ca(NO_3)_2$, LiCl

8   Clockwise from top right: burette, pure water, accurately weighed solid sample, titration flask, acid or alkali

9   **a** $NaOH + HCl \rightarrow NaCl + H_2O$
    b $2KOH + H_2SO_4 \rightarrow K_2SO_4 + 2H_2O$
    c $2Mg + O_2 \rightarrow 2MgO$
    d $4Li + O_2 \rightarrow 2Li_2O$
    e $AgNO_3 + NaCl \rightarrow AgCl + NaNO_3$
    f $Pb(NO_3)_2 + 2KCl \rightarrow PbCl_2 + 2KNO_3$
    g $2Fe_2O_3 + 3C \rightarrow 3CO_2 + 4Fe$
    h $CaCO_3 \rightarrow CaO + CO_2$

10 **a**   metal   **b**   salt + water
    c   salt   **d**   water + carbon dioxide
    e $2HNO_3(aq) + Na_2CO_3(s) \rightarrow 2NaNO_3(aq) + CO_2(g) + H_2O(l)$
    f $H_2SO_4(aq) + 2KOH(aq) \rightarrow K_2SO_4(aq) + 2H_2O(l)$
    g $H_2SO_4(aq) + CaO(s) \rightarrow CaSO_4(aq) + H_2O(l)$

h $2HCl(aq) + Mg(s) \rightarrow MgCl_2(aq) + H_2(g)$

a	h
b	f
c	g
d	e

11 a slower **b** faster **c** faster

d slower **e** can't tell **f** can't tell

12 From left to right: B C A

13 a **i** 36.5 **ii** 84 **iii** 95 **iv** 44 **v** 18

b Reacting masses: 71 g, 84 g, 95 g, 44 g, 18 g

c 47.5 g

14 SrO – 94 %, Al_2O_3 – 99 %, SF_6 – 93 %

15 1 dessicator, 2 crystallization, 3 end point, 4 catalyst, 5 hydroxide, 6 slower, 7 sulfuric, 8 nitrate, 9 salt

C6 GCSE-style questions

1 a H_2SO_4 – sulfuric acid, NaOH – sodium hydroxide, NaCl – sodium chloride, Na_2CO_3 – sodium carbonate

b **i** Liquid

ii It is corrosive and harmful

c Flavouring food – 99.0 %, mixing with grit to put on icy roads – 90.0 %, in a saline drip for a hospital patient – 99.99 %

2 a **i** $2HCl(aq) + CaCO_3(s) \rightarrow CaCl_2(aq) + CO_2(g)$
$+ H_2O(l)$

ii Goes up

b **i** Decreases – carbon dioxide gas escapes from the reaction mixture

ii It gets faster. This is because molecules have a greater chance of colliding in a more concentrated solution. More collisions in a certain time means the reaction is faster.

iii Do the reaction at a lower temperature; use bigger lumps of calcium carbonate.

3 a A F D B C E

b **i** water

ii $H^+ + OH^- \rightarrow H_2O$

iii Citric acid

4 a 201 kg **b** 320 kg **c** 490 g

5 a Stir . . . – to make sure the reactants mix together well; filter . . . – to separate the solution from the excess powder; heat . . . – to evaporate most of the water; cool . . . – to evaporate the rest of the water.

b 80 %

P6 Workout

1 Vibrations are at right angles . . . – transverse – x-rays, water waves and waves on a rope; vibrations are in the same direction . . . – longitudinal – sound waves. Other answers possible.

2 Wave – a disturbance moving through a material medium – the material a wave travels through; frequency – the number of waves a source makes every second; source – this vibrates to make a wave.

3 See diagram on page 155.

4 a 333 m/s **b** 0.333 km/s

5 A – refraction; B – diffraction; C – reflection

6 a 2 m/s **b** 340 m/s

7 Reinforce, constructive, B, cancel out, destructive, A

8 a 1500 m **b** 0.6 m

9 Frequency, speed, wavelength, refraction, faster, towards

10 a

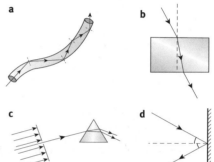

11 Digital signals transmit information with higher quality than analogue signals. This is because noise can be removed from digital signals but not from analogue signals.

12 1 radio, 2 infrared, 3 frequency, 4 variation, 5 receiver, 6 AM, 7 analogue, 8 digital, 9 interference, 10 decode, 11 – noise

P6 GCSE-style questions

1 a

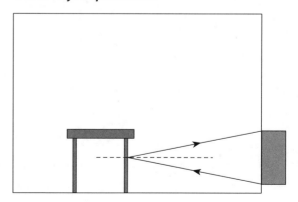

b C

c 10 000 000 000

d Microwaves are reflected by metal

2 a Amplitude = 30 m; frequency = 2 waves per hour; wavelength = 3 km

b i

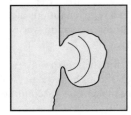

　　ii Diffraction

c i Refraction

　　ii Arrow at right angles to crests of waves in shallow water

3 a Top – AM; middle – digital; bottom – FM

b B E D C A

c With digital signals, 0 and 1 can still be recognized even if noise has been picked up. So the signal can be 'cleaned up' by removing the noise. Noise cannot be removed from analogue signals.

4 a Transmitted

b Absorbs – If the intensity of the light that comes out of the brain is less than expected, the brain might be bleeding. This suggests that blood absorbs light, so the intensity of transmitted light decreases.

c In one second, a different number of photons arrives at each detector.

d i One of: X-rays damage living cells and can cause cancer; X-rays will be absorbed by the bone of the skull, so will give no useful information.

　　ii Microwaves have a heating effect, so will heat up brain tissue causing great damage.

index

Index